College Gpa

Steps to Achieve Success in Your Academic Life

(A Comprehensive Guide to Achieving the Perfect College Gpa)

Bernard Sawyer

Published By **Bella Frost**

Bernard Sawyer

All Rights Reserved

College Gpa: Steps to Achieve Success in Your Academic Life (A Comprehensive Guide to Achieving the Perfect College Gpa)

ISBN   978-1-7753142-3-3

No part of this guidebook shall be reproduced in any form without permission in writing from the publisher except in the case of brief quotations embodied in critical articles or reviews.

Legal & Disclaimer

The information contained in this book is not designed to replace or take the place of any form of medicine or professional medical advice. The information in this book has been provided for educational & entertainment purposes only.

The information contained in this book has been compiled from sources deemed reliable, and it is accurate to the best of the Author's knowledge; however, the Author cannot guarantee its accuracy and validity and cannot be held liable for any errors or omissions. Changes are periodically made to this book. You must consult your doctor or get professional medical advice before using any of the suggested remedies, techniques, or information in this book.

Upon using the information contained in this book, you agree to hold harmless the Author from and against any damages, costs, and expenses, including any legal fees potentially resulting from the application of any of the information provided by this guide. This disclaimer applies to any damages or injury caused by the use and application, whether directly or indirectly, of any advice or information presented, whether for breach of contract, tort, negligence, personal injury, criminal intent, or under any other cause of action.

You agree to accept all risks of using the information presented inside this book. You need to consult a professional medical practitioner in order to ensure you are both able and healthy enough to participate in this program.

Table Of Contents

Chapter 1: Record Your Whole Schedule . 1

Chapter 2: Develop Flash Memory 10

Chapter 3: Memorize With Mnemonics . 23

Chapter 4: Accept Your Laziness To Be Less Lazy 33

Chapter 5: Group Work 46

Chapter 6: Tips That Couldn't Be Forced Into Other Categories 60

Chapter 7: Skip Class Sparingly 77

Chapter 8: Major Ideas 82

Chapter 9: Things You Will Realize After College That You Can Learn Now Instead 93

Chapter 10: Making The Most Of Lectures 105

Chapter 11: Staying On Track 119

Chapter 12: How To Mastermind A Feasible Plan 135

Chapter 13: Getting The Grades 148

Chapter 14: Choose Your Professors Wisely 160

Chapter 15: Attend Class Consistently . 171

Chapter 16: Take Prolific Notes............ 178

Chapter 1: Record Your Whole Schedule

AT THE BEGINNING OF EACH QUARTER or semester, make an effort to record assignments, due dates, and check dates on an without problem handy calendar or planner. A complete-year calendar that may be hung on your wall is a high-quality desire. Another opportunity is to lessen out the months for the region or semester from a month-to-month calendar so that you can see everything right now.

The above method may be in fact beneficial, because of the fact you may see what's bobbing up and plan it gradual as a end result. There is a considerably large difference in perspective amongst looking at a month-to-month calendar and being able to see the complete region or semester . Also, if there's not a few aspect to do or no character around, you is probably stimulated to look in advance and knock out a few art work that allows you to spend it sluggish in greater fun methods.

Many college college college students will choose to apply a calendar solution on a smartphone, tablet or computer, options that also can art work properly, in particular for university students who're not often domestic. As with all recommendations in this ebook, you want to find out what works nice for you, but if you're locating which you're getting in the back of on paintings due to the fact you're not aware of what's developing, it could be definitely truly worth considering the each 12 months calendar idea.

Study If You're Bored to Feel Bored and Productive

TRY TO USE YOUR DOWN intervals to get earlier. Admittedly, the ones are the times at the same time as you won't need to art work, however I'm no longer talking approximately vacations, or usually even weekends. I'm talking approximately times sooner or later of the day at the same time as no individual else is spherical and you're looking TV or sitting round on campus. Keep your books reachable with the intention to do get art work completed at some point of these periods. You should do math issues you recognise a way to do, or acquire studies substances for an upcoming paper. If you're in advance of the game due to the truth you acquire art work finished for the duration of uninteresting instances, you'll be able to loosen up and experience the a laugh times.

Do the Work to Lose the Anxiety

WORRYING DOESN'T RELIEVE ANXIETY. Action does. Break subjects into small quantities and chip away at them. If the massive image is simply too overwhelming, simply take a look at a undertaking grade by grade. If it's however too overwhelming, ruin it down even in addition.

Starting a task is typically the toughest issue for maximum people. A specific remedy for such procrastination is to installation your homework or project as soon as feasible. For some reason, getting taking area a venture seems to be a whole lot less difficult if 1% is finished in region of if not anything has been started. Even if it's a twenty-net page paper, begin thru writing the pick out, your name and date. You can stop there, or very likely, you'll realize that because the step most effective took a minute, you also have time to install writing out a difficult define and probably some initial thoughts. You may apprehend that you may do a piece greater at that difficulty, and earlier than you realize it, you've made giant progress.

Momentum is produced from a series of small steps, so allow this strain paintings to your pick with the useful resource of putting topics in motion early.

Plan Free Time to Have More of It

PLAN YOUR "FREE" TIME AS a outstanding deal as you intend your reading. We can simplest attention on one detail for goodbye, and it's applicable to take take a look at breaks. If you're faced with a venture that appears overwhelming, undergo in thoughts now not handiest taking have a study breaks, but making plans them in advance of time.

The above technique absolutely relies upon on your artwork style, despite the fact that. If you're a "marathoner," taking a spoil may additionally kill your precious momentum; if you're a "sprinter," taking a brief, amusing break could be all you want to regain your electricity and energy thru the rest of the paintings.

Also, working for a finite quantity of time seems loads much less disturbing than running for an open-ended quantity of time. Be cautious of searching TV or playing video video video video games in a few unspecified time in the future of any breaks, despite the fact that, or you will probably sap your energy. Go for a walk out of doors, shoot a few hoops, or have a moderate snack. Most importantly, set a time to get lower again to artwork so you can regain your consciousness rapid.

Rein in Electronic Communication Time

YOU MIGHT WANT TO CONSIDER checking your e mail best a couple of times consistent with day and putting remaining dates for social media and texting. Tim Ferriss has a notable dialogue on time-wasters in his #1 excellent-promoting e-book, The 4-Hour Workweek. He shows checking e-mail two times in step with day at pre-set instances.

Email, social media and texting are such a part of the existence now that they are tough to avoid, but they can also waste numerous time. If you've got have been given a big amount of exertions to do, it is probably useful at instances to stay offline and to turn your telephone off. Another brilliant technique is to take care of any electronic conversation at the same time as you best have a brief quantity of time amongst instructions.

Choose to Not Connect on Last-Minute Scrambling

MAKING CONNECTIONS WITH OTHERS ON healthy shared hobbies (together with sports activities sports or pastimes) is an critical a part of lifestyles. People furthermore be a part of on horrible things, in spite of the truth that, and this kind of is procrastination. Many university college students wear procrastination like a badge of honor, bragging approximately how past due they waited to do a paper and the manner they have been up late all night time time doing it. People enjoy being attentive to this, due to the reality lots of them waited till the final 2nd, too, and it makes them enjoy higher if others are in the equal boat. Is it better to healthy on this way, or to get a mission achieved multiple days early and be able to do what you want?

Rise above the false sense of connection and feel the relief of completing a project early. Better however, encourage friends to get their art work executed early so they'll have extra free time as nicely.

Maximizing Study Time: When, Where and How

Choose Where You Study Based on Your Goals

WHERE YOU STUDY CAN BE very vital. Introverts may additionally find out this to be actual extra than extraverts, as introverts have a tendency to be extra with out hassle distracted by way of the use of way of subjects together with noise, but even extraverts can gain from fewer distractions. If you want to take a look at with people to get to apprehend them higher, glide for it, however you could need to time table time beyond law to have a have a have a look at for your very very own if analyzing with others distracts you from gaining knowledge of.

Go in the direction of the grain to locate effective instances and places to examine. Go to the library early on a weekend night time time, or early on Saturday or Sunday morning whilst most human beings are despite the fact that asleep. Empty classrooms additionally can be tremendous places to have a examine. Be creative in terms of in which you test, due to the truth the more modern your idea, the an entire lot tons much less likely others are using it, resulting in much less distractions for you.

Chapter 2: Develop Flash Memory

FLASH CARDS CAN BE A amazing analyzing tool, but there are multiple guidelines to maintain in thoughts an excellent manner to apply them efficaciously. Students will regularly create a massive stack of playing cards to memorize and go through the stack time and again on the manner to examine the terms and thoughts. There's a better way.

After you guess the solution on every card, mark down on the lower lower lower back how nicely you knew the solution. An clean manner to do this is to mark every "Y" for Yes (you obtain the answer effects), "M" for Maybe (unsure till you looked at the solution), or "N" for No (no concept). The second time spherical, mark the playing cards once more. If you mark a card "Y" for a second time, get rid of the card from the deck, as the solution has sunk in. Repeat those steps till you get a "Y" times in a row for every card (or 3 times in case you're extra cautious).

A greater green version of the above method is to be honest with yourself about the answers you in truth comprehend, and throwing the gambling playing cards with those solutions to the aspect right away. By the usage of the second method, you could slim the playing cards to those you're having trouble guessing correctly extra short.

If high quality playing cards take you numerous tries to get proper, preserve them in a separate pile on the way to assessment them yet again fast right in advance than the test.

Many college college students undergo complete decks of flash playing playing cards time and again, but you'll possibly find the method described above will prevent time and beautify your retention of hard test topics.

Think of Whether Study Groups Work for You

SEPARATE STUDY TIME FROM SOCIAL time. Study businesses may be useful, but many offer best a bit studying together with quite some social interplay. Be honest with yourself about whether or not you look at subjects higher in a collection. If you do examine better in a hard and fast, then determine out at what factor finally of the studying cycle this is actual. For example, do you benefit a higher keep close on requirements to begin with in a tough and rapid, or does a hard and fast putting help organization up what you've located out (via imparting the opportunity to ask about what you don't recognize and supporting others with what you do apprehend)? Also, whilst comparing the usefulness of a have a look at group, make sure to don't forget the amount of time spent in relation to what is completed.

Sense the Sense That Makes Sense for You

FIGURE OUT YOUR LEARNING STYLE after which make the high-quality use of it. How do you "get" subjects exceptional? By being attentive to the professor and no longer having the distraction of taking notes? By taking massive notes? By copying the notes you took in beauty a 2nd time? By studying? By schooling others?

If you're no longer positive which experience works high-quality for you in terms of mastering, strive some of the above strategies in an clean class. Be careful not to check one in every of a type studying techniques with the resource of doing some difficulty like now not taking notes in a hard elegance and then understanding how caught you are whilst it's time for the primary check. Pay attention to what works for you in desire to simply doing what all and sundry else seems to be doing.

If you're actually now not splendid what your getting to know fashion is, enter the terms "gaining expertise of style," or something similar, online and also you'll discover hundreds of links explaining specific getting to know styles at the aspect of self-tests that will help you find out what works tremendous for you.

Use Words for Number Problem Problems

IF YOU GET TO A difficult problem, especially in a topic including math or physics wherein there's one correct answer, attempt writing out in terms what you don't comprehend (i.E., what is making you caught). Then, write out what you'll need to understand or do to be able to get beyond it.

You should make tough issues seem much less overwhelming using this approach, due to the reality you are breaking the problem down into what you could do and what's inflicting you to get stuck. For example, you might write, "there are three variables, only one is thought, and I don't realize the manner to discover one of the missing variables." Then, you may write that capacity solutions are as follows: 1) call Dave from magnificence; 2) go to professor's place of job hours; 3) scour the e-book; four) try a web search for a comparable hassle. If you can't find a solution proper away, circulate straight away to the issues you can do and get once more to the tough ones later. You can also see in case you keep jogging up closer to the same limitations or if a next hassle lets in you apprehend what you've got been missing earlier than.

Focus to Get More Done Quicker

ONE OF THE MOST IMPORTANT capabilities that must be self-taught is the potential of sustained focus. Being able to get artwork completed however distractions is a brilliant capacity to increase, and interest is a completely important ability to have for tough issues.

These thoughts would possibly probable seem self-apparent, but how often do humans clearly offer interest to 1 trouble for extra than approximately ten mins with out distractions? Focused attention is how huge problems are solved, whether or not inner a tough and rapid or by using using an man or woman. Not simplest are the answers that pop out of focused artwork frequently higher, but interest additionally abilities as a time-saver. Try to find out a quiet corner of the top ground of the library or a few distinctive spot in that you recognize you could constantly attention on the equal time as wanted, and you can find out that artwork that used to take you a couple of hours may be completed in a half of of-hour.

Don't Study As Much As Others... or More Than Others

SET YOUR OWN STANDARDS FOR studying. Be cautious not to fall right right into a trap of basing how a amazing deal you want to have a look at on how lots one-of-a-type human beings are analyzing. This is a lure for a few motives. First of all, a few human beings are quite clever and don't want to observe masses. Second, some people don't care tons about their grades and don't take a look at a whole lot. Third, you don't see each person man or woman all of the time, and a few humans observe at ordinary instances. Lastly, a few human beings may additionally although be stuck up in the concept that reading isn't cool and sneak off to do it. Base your efforts on what's required for every magnificence and your non-public dreams. Let your grades, now not the efforts of others, be the diploma of whether or not or now not you're doing enough.

Reduce Clutter to Reduce Stress

DOES CLUTTER REALLY CAUSE STRESS, or absolutely upload to it? That's debatable, but there surely seems to be a courting amongst muddle and pressure. If you don't keep in mind it, consider getting some paintings carried out even as you're in a cluttered room, and then recall the identical work once more an hour later while you've wiped easy the room. Does it feel a bit precise? Maybe even plenty extraordinary? Physical space could have an effect on how we experience mentally. Clearing up clutter offers a experience of region and may take the brink off of overwhelming feelings that would rise up while you're confronted with a large venture. The greater obvious blessings are being capable of discover your papers and having enough room to art work!

Learn By Teaching

LEARN BY TEACHING OTHERS. Make sure you draw close the material first (or as a minimum be sincere about what you don't understand). Teaching can be a outstanding way to get fabric to sink in better, and additionally to discern out if there are areas in which you though want a few brushing up. You also can do a alternate via manner of coaching a subject you understand truely properly to a scholar who can in flip assist you with some specific assignment.

Learn Using Headphones

READING ISN'T ALWAYS FEASIBLE OR safe in tremendous situations, however the time you spend within the ones conditions doesn't need to be wasted. Try recording the most vital notes for a test and being attentive to them for your automobile or on the bus. If you file your notes for a check a terrific way to be aware of them, you're no longer simplest making use of greater time that could otherwise be wasted, but you're also learning from a couple of angles. First, you concentrate the professor in beauty and write down the notes. Next, you need to examine the notes out loud that allows you to file them. Finally, you pay attention them over again at the recording.

It will take the time to report the notes, however thru the use of time you in any other case wouldn't be capable of use for studying, and through technique of creating yourself take a look at thru writing, analyzing, and listening (times!), you'll have a much better threat of soaking up the material. Of direction, in case you don't have as lots time, a much extra direct method can be to in reality tape a lecture and take note of it inside the locations described above, despite the fact that this technique wouldn't embody as many varieties of mastering.

Three

Go Ahead, Test Me

Use Study Guides with Confidence... Usually

TRUST, BUT VERIFY, THE ACCURACY of look at courses. In maximum commands, test courses truely do distill the hassle do not forget into all that wants to be studied for a specific test, in spite of the reality that some professors stray from what they embody in a have a take a look at guide. Speak with beyond university college college students about how your professor operates, or look for online reviews of professors, specifically if opinions are available for your unique class.

I obtained a painful lesson about have a look at courses in my first actual region of college. I depended on that a have a have a look at guide in a specific splendor may additionally want to effectively reflect what might be on the take a look at, however unluckily that wasn't the case the least bit. Even worse, I was no longer conscious that the professor on this unique splendor had been using the exact equal take a look at for numerous years. Consequently, some of the members of fraternities and sororities in the beauty had copies of the take a look at. These college college students drove up the curve due to the truth they all have been given such high rankings. (On a tangential be aware, people of fraternities and sororities can be very good resources of records about lessons and professors because of the truth they are able to skip down statistics in a non-prevent circulate every 12 months.)

I determined my terrible revel in in that one magnificence to be the exception, notwithstanding the truth that. In maximum commands, the take a look at guides were very correct outlines of what is probably on a check. Just make certain to test with the professor, critiques, current university college students, or past college students to confirm.

Chapter 3: Memorize With Mnemonics

MAKE USE OF MNEMONIC DEVICES in getting prepared for checks. Mnemonics are effects memorable, catchy sentences wherein each first letter suits the primary letter of what you need to memorize. The trick proper here is to make certain there's a few element about the phrase you operate for you to in truth help you endure in thoughts the word. The best way to do this is to have the number one letters of the word fit in preference to simply the number one letter. For example, use the phrase "normally" to symbolize Alabama. If you most effective in form the primary letter, it may quite a bit more tough to bear in thoughts which word the artificial is meant to represent.

If you don't need to go to the hassle of making up your very very own mnemonic gadgets, you can do an internet are in search of to without trouble discover many possibilities for common principles. For instance, Wikipedia presently has an entire web web page devoted to chemistry mnemonics.

Crack the Code

TRY TO FIGURE OUT THE political and philosophical biases of professors. These biases often come through in lectures and inside the wording of questions about tests (and in solutions on multiple preference assessments). The books a professor assigns also can provide clues. Don't look for biases too difficult within the occasion that they're no longer at the surface, however once in a while it's pretty easy to pick up some greater elements on a take a look at at the same time as biases are recognized. Just records that university professors generally tend closer to political correctness can upload some elements on every test in a few instructions, mainly in political generation and history.

Retain Tests for Future Gains

IF POSSIBLE, KEEP YOUR MIDTERMS as a manner to assessment them for finals. Each professor has a wonderful style, and browsing again over a take a look at will let you consider what sorts of questions had been requested. You also can see if you may spot any specific styles, particularly in more than one preference assessments. Was "all the above" the precise solution in seven out of the 8 questions wherein it seemed? If so, it's possibly a superb guess on questions for that you're unsure of the answer. Does the longest solution will be inclined to be correct? Multiple choice assessments often offer many strategies to "crack the code" if you could dedicate a while to investigating patterns inside the solution alternatives.

Some professors create higher checks than others, and you can advantage a huge benefit thru searching out patterns in early assessments a good way to do better because the time period is going on. If you're not allowed to preserve a midterm, at least you may commonly see the test on the day it's again and make be aware about as plenty as viable about the questions and solutions whilst the professor is going over the test in beauty.

Effectively Tackle Scantron® Tests

IF YOU ARE ALLOWED TO write on a test's query sheet, burst off answers you recognize for sure are wrong. In order to take the take a look at faster, you can mark your solutions on the actual check the first time through, after which transfer them to the solution shape in some time. If an answer, circle it on the question sheet and bypass on. If you don't recognize the answer on a specific question, go off the answers are wrong and flow into on. Don't spend too much time on any man or woman question the number one time via the take a look at.

On the second time thru, transfer your solutions to the Scantron® shape as you circulate alongside, starting with those you already grew to grow to be around, and making your excellent guesses at the others. (If you've got were given plenty of time, an exceptional better method is to undergo a 2d time to mark all of your answers at the check sheet, and then to transport lower again a 3rd time to replace each approach to the answer sheet.) Be nice to hold a watch consistent at the clock with the intention to have time to exchange solutions. Another benefit to this technique is that it's going to assist you avoid the not unusual problem of getting answers at the Scantron® form no longer suit up with the questions about the take a look at sheet because of skipped answers.

Don't Cheat, Even If Cheaters Sometimes Win

DON'T CHEAT. JUST DON'T do it. The best person to whom it must remember whether or not or now not you "get away" with dishonest is your self, meaning that in truth you by no means escape with it. Keep your integrity in take a look at and use the gear from this ebook to do properly on checks irrespective of what different university college college students do to raise the curve with the aid of dishonest. If you want a more practical reason, don't do it due to the truth a C on a take a look at is better than the consequences of having caught, which may be a 0 on a check at pleasant, or very probable, expulsion.

Avoid Temptation During Crucial Times

YOU WILL BENEFIT FROM KEEPING your surroundings predictable in advance than a take a look at. Try going off to a quiet a part of the library or turning into a member of up with a have a observe organisation to move over the test. If you're mainly prone to being distracted with the useful resource of manner of video games, partying, or some component else with a view to make your thinking hazy, plan in advance to keep away from such temptations. Planning what you'll do for a few hours leading as much as a take a look at will help offer peace of mind. The remaining element you'll want is to enjoy aggravating about what may also upward push up that could have an impact at the manner you do. Schedule a time and location to be throughout the time important as plenty as a check, irrespective of what else may possibly take place, and also you'll located your self within the right body of thoughts to do your tremendous.

Avoid the Convenient Excuse Trap

DON'T SKIP STUDYING THE NIGHT in advance than a check that allows you to have an excuse for yourself and others for why you got a lousy grade. If you preserve your ears open, you'll see sincerely how commonplace the ones excuses are. It can also sound corny, however it surely takes courage to try your first-rate. If you take a look at difficult and fail, it can be a blow in your ego. If you go to a celebration as a substitute, you can clearly persuade yourself and others how a whole lot better you'll have done had you studied.

You can be tempted to see what you could pull off with raw intelligence, and you can do thoroughly. Just recognize that the top people in any area almost continually art work tough on pinnacle of getting expertise. Our culture appears to be desirous approximately herbal abilties, but it doesn't get humans some distance except they exercise. Put within the effort and time to acquire success and you may marvel yourself with how plenty you could achieve.

Prepare for Admissions Exams

WHETHER YOU WILL BE TAKING the SAT to get into an undergraduate utility or a take a look at like the GMAT to get right proper right into a graduate software, make use of each useful aid you may to put together for the check. Any bookstore should have numerous alternatives of books that can be used as look at belongings, and those books are well worth the time, specially once they embody exercising assessments. Do each exercise check you can, whilst preserving the surroundings and time recommendations as near as feasible to what you'll enjoy whilst you're taking the real take a look at. Don't prevent taking the exercising checks until you may score even higher than your intention and you could get the take a look at completed in an awful lot much less time than required, as it's very likely you acquired't be quite as cushty throughout the actual take a look at irrespective of how lots coaching you do.

Other resources to hold in mind, if you could manipulate to pay for them, are education and private tutors. If you're capable of use the ones sources, specially personal tutors, you might be capable of accelerate your getting to know system and acquire a terrific better rating. Also, if you have an auditory getting to know style, taking a category might be greater powerful for you than using a ebook.

No count which approach you use to prepare for admissions check, ensure you do put together appreciably, as particular strategies do exist for each take a look at that you may use to accumulate a bump up on your rating.

Accept Your Laziness to Get More Done

Chapter 4: Accept Your Laziness To Be Less Lazy

DISCIPLINE IS A VALUABLE TRAIT, and getting your art work finished regardless of the manner you sense is one of the maximum vital look at behavior. Therefore, preventing laziness with all of your would likely could appear a profitable effort. However, such attempt can reason stepped forward resistance. Instead, be given that your goals have a lazy component to them. Why does this mentality paintings? Because it's human nature to need to get as masses completed as feasible with as little art work! If you wait to art work hard until you need to art work difficult, you're now not probably to get a amazing deal done. In fact, the urge to paintings hard might not ever come. Accept that you're lazy and do the artwork besides. There's no need to waste time and strength seeking to persuade your self which you're now not lazy. Viewing yourself as a hard employee isn't a prerequisite to getting a number of artwork completed.

During the times on the identical time as you don't have the energy to paintings tough to get lots finished, and also you're now not up closer to a critical remaining date, take shipping of your lack of electricity and get a hint achieved in vicinity of fighting it and not getting something executed the least bit. At least that is a amazing approach in a few times, essential us to the subsequent element about distinct varieties of reading.

Study Differently for Different Circumstances

LEARN TO DIFFERENTIATE BETWEEN TYPES of studying as a way to make green use of a while. For example, you might be capable of make flash gambling cards whilst looking TV, however you could probable need a quiet surroundings to memorize the flash playing playing cards. You is probably capable of knock out easy math troubles if you're already acquainted with them, but you'll possibly need to attention that allows you to study new mind. Think about what the intention of a test consultation is, and you've got were given at the manner to figure out the great form of surroundings wherein to finish the art work.

Pay Attention to Your Energy Patterns

NOTE THE TIMES OF DAY or conditions in which you do and don't have energy. This announcement will help with each training and analyzing. Try to avoid taking hard, boring classes inside the afternoon if you commonly enjoy sleepy at that element (as many do). If you keep in mind your electricity styles while you check in for training, you'll probable discover that you have an less complicated time in elegance and analyzing out of doors of class.

Study When You Will Instead of When You Should

WHEN ARE YOU REALLY WILLING to look at? Doing some factor mellow the night time time earlier than a massive take a look at day is a tremendous idea, but fooling yourself into wondering you'll study throughout a time while you've in no way been powerful not frequently works. If you may have a look at on weekend nights, that's outstanding, as the ones is probably the quietest times via an extended way in locations similar to the library, but don't omit out on a social lifestyles actually if you're not virtually going to get an entire lot finished anyway. While this ebook focuses mostly on grades, "who " has a tendency to count quite a chunk when applying for jobs and internships, so make certain to growth as many pinnacle connections as you may on the equal time as you're in college.

Set Deadlines to Feel Less Stress

TRY SETTING A DEADLINE A few days in advance than your due date, and don't pressure till that point. You won't waste as a good deal time stressing yourself out approximately procrastinating in case you recognize the date thru that you want to start. Write down what wishes to be executed, and lists duties to be able to paintings backwards, setting small closing dates along the way. Don't ruin your weekends via worrying approximately art work you weren't going to do till Monday night time time besides. Enjoy your unfastened time as an alternative, understanding that the art work gets executed brief.

By the use of the approach described above, you'll gain the intellectual benefit of know-how you don't ought to get the paintings completed till a sure factor. The trick is that it is able to be an lousy lot much less complex to get art work finished if we feel like we don't must get it completed, and of direction in case you experience like doing more artwork earlier of time, it will handiest benefit you. Nothing is as relaxing as finishing an project early after which not having to worry approximately it in any respect.

Act First to Feel Motivated

MOTIVATION COMES FROM ACTION, and no longer the other way spherical. If you wait to act until you're recommended, you would possibly never save you prepared! As extraordinary-selling author Robert Ringer stated in his ebook, Action: Nothing Happens Until Something Moves, "Contrary to famous belief, you don't need to be brought approximately to act. If crucial, strain your self to obtain this, and motivation could have a examine."

The idea of beginning paintings will not regularly sound appealing, but stepping into the go with the go with the flow of hard work can genuinely be interesting, and completing artwork continually feels proper. We normally generally tend to magnify how horrible artwork is probably in our minds, but then as soon as we start on something it's often no longer as horrific as we feared, and that's while the inducement and energy begin to pick up. Sometimes motivation gained't come the least bit, and you simply should grit your tooth and paintings via an challenge. If motivation is to head back, you regularly acquired't understand until you've already started operating, so certainly get commenced and notice if that extra decorate will help you get your work finished.

Develop Discipline Instead of Worrying About Motivation

CONCERN YOURSELF WITH BEING DISCIPLINED in preference to being stimulated. Motivation comes and goes and is tough to manipulate. The maximum green human beings are disciplined. They do what they need to do whether or not they revel in love it or now not, and actually, they understand that it's often what they sense like doing the least if you want to offer the greatest advantages over the long time. Natural motivation is great, however no longer essential, and realistically it may not ever come.

Be cautious no longer to have a look at an excessive amount of into loss of motivation. For instance, you could now not be inspired to do your biology homework, but this lack of motivation doesn't always imply you don't want to be a medical medical doctor. (On the alternative hand, in case you volunteer in a clinic and hate it, this experience might be some aspect to be privy to.)

In existence, problem can be the most critical skills to make bigger. People stay in shape due to their vicinity regarding eating conduct and exercising, they turn out to be professional in a musical tool from disciplined exercise, and they beautify in their careers from the world it takes to get the procedure finished. The in advance you may expand this vital ability, the more effective you'll be, and the less difficult it will likely be to have subject spill over to notable areas of your lifestyles. Discipline is largely a depend of exercising, so art work at it the equal manner you'd paintings at growing each other learned ability.

Use Small Amounts of Time to Achieve Big Results

LOOK FOR UNCOMMON TIMES TO do homework. You is probably amazed to find out how loads more reading you could % in if you get a bit innovative. Some capacity places to get more test time in are at a baseball (general time period), on the bus, in lengthy lines, on the laundromat, within the cafeteria, outside on the grass, at the beach, and in a class in advance than it begins offevolved. Some times to don't forget are early in advance than everybody else is huge extensive awake, early Friday night time time while you're geared up to go out, any time you're ready to fulfill up with someone, and at half of-time at notable wearing sports.

Bring artwork with you on every occasion there's any danger of having a while to fill so you don't bypass over out. For instance, you can carry a paperback from an English magnificence with you if you're going to the publish workplace or medical doctor's workplace in which the wait can be an hour or greater. Think about what form of art work you is probably capable of do in high quality conditions, and plan ahead to make the most of ability possibilities.

Use Parkinson's Law to Your Advantage

PARKINSON'S LAW STATES THAT "WORK expands so that you can fill the time to be had for its crowning glory." This regulation can be used very successfully. When have a observe time is open-ended, and no longer some issue is scheduled in some time, it can be very traumatic, as it without a doubt looks as if there may be no result in sight.

Consequently, university students often procrastinate in such conditions, because of the reality the venture seems too daunting. However, there can be an opportunity, and you could discover it very effective, even though it seems quite simple on the floor.

One software program of Parkinson's Law to analyzing is probably to discover wallet of time proper earlier than some component amusing is scheduled. If you've got were given have been given an hour (or perhaps 20 mins) earlier than a celebration, or a exercising, or certainly anything you're searching forward to, use that issue to get in a few short analyzing. The ache can be over in advance than you understand it, and also you'll be so targeted to get to the a laugh event that you could locate you're hundreds extra green than traditional throughout this time.

Although a hint special from Parkinson's Law, a few other way you can use the tension of an expected event in your benefit is to set a selected quantity of work to get carried out and to now not go to the occasion you're searching forward to until that work is completed. Then you'll actually attention!

Record How You Spend Your Time

CONSIDER RECORDING WHAT YOU DO every hour of each day for each week. This is an immoderate step, and I can quite plenty assure it's the satisfactory that only a few readers will simply do. But if you're inclined to make an effort to do it for best one week, it's miles succesful that will help you now not handiest in college, however for the relaxation of your life. Why? Because you'll see how masses loose time you without a doubt do have. And agree with me, except you're jogging 40 hours and taking 20 devices, you likely have masses extra free time than you observed.

If you sleep eight hours a night time time, that interprets to snoozing fifty six hours out of a total of 168 hours within the route of the week. That leaves 112 waking hours at some point of the week. Take away 20 hours of commands consistent with week from present day waking hours, and the stability is 92 hours. Take away hours in step with day for consuming and hygiene for a complete of 14 hours in step with week, and that leaves seventy eight hours. That's quite some time! It's proper, or even critical, to use some of those hours for rest and rest. If you discover your self killing time in vicinity of spending it productively, despite the fact that, you'll see how plenty greater you may get done by manner of figuring out what a while wasters are and limiting them in desire of greater powerful activities.

Chapter 5: Group Work

Draft Your Team Wisely

BE VERY SELECTIVE WHEN CHOOSING a crew for employer projects (if given the choice). Not handiest will being selective in deciding on a set help you get better grades, however it may additionally assist hold your relationships. A super friend won't placed out plenty attempt in employer situations, straining your relationship with that man or woman. If you're uncertain about the way to cope with now not seeking to art work with a chum, really inform that person you recognize too many pals who had their relationships stricken by being in companies collectively, and that being friends is extra critical than being on the equal institution. Your friend would in all likelihood nonetheless be get rid of and expect you're creating a big deal out of not something, however this even though is probably higher than risking an entire semester of hysteria.

Scout Potential Group Members

IF YOU ASK AROUND, YOU might be able to find out who works nicely in corporations and who does no longer. This records may be very valuable! In programs that require a number of business enterprise paintings, analyzing the reputations of others is reasonably clean. The secret's to discover about the extremes, that means who's the remarkable in corporations and who's the worst. By going for walks difficult and doing a super activity on organisation initiatives early on your self, you could increase a strong recognition as well as perfect relationships with unique sturdy students who will need to paintings with you all over again. If you're capable of discover a robust middle group of ability group people, you could even plan to take education collectively wherein you understand you'll be capable of select your personal organization.

Grind It Out

WORK IN GROUPS IS RARELY disbursed flippantly. A pupil used to getting C's knows that by using way of turning into a member of a group with A-college college students, she or he is probably able to do C artwork and however get as a minimum a B. The A-college students might be disenchanted, however the C-scholar will get a B for doing C art work. Sometimes professors allow college students to grade others internal their organization anonymously. Even then, a few university students truely don't care, or even being graded in my view by means of using their teammates obtained't inspire them to paintings tough. At instances it's simplest a rely of placing your head down and getting via project or magnificence. Keep in mind the stop motive of having the extraordinary grade feasible and don't get too stuck up about what is sincere.

Consider Working as Just One Man or Just One Woman

FOR THE REASONS IN THE closing segment, you can choose out to avoid group art work whilst possible if you want greater manage over your grades. Classes with enterprise organization work frequently come to be taking greater of it slow as well. Exceptions exist, however among coordinating a mission, ineffectively seeking to get artwork completed in the course of meetings, after which looking to piece the assignment together, company tasks can take an inordinate amount of it sluggish. Also, because of the truth companies generally meet more than crucial, and it's tough to discover times at the same time as each person is free, you'll have much less manipulate over your free time, as any time you have got had been given loose is anticipated to be available for conferences.

Test Early and Be Thankful Later

CONSIDER GIVING EACH MEMBER OF your organization a quick venture as early as feasible to gauge virtually all and sundry's paintings ethic and incredible of exertions while there can be even though time to modify organization roles. If you may parent out the relative strengths and weaknesses of simply really anybody early on, you'll be able to amplify a remarkable approach to mitigate weaknesses. It's a bargain less difficult to address capability weaknesses on the start of the area or semester than to be surprised with the aid of the usage of them right in advance than a assignment is due. On a greater great word, you'll possibly find out some very robust skills in a quiet or humble company member that may be located to loads higher use than if assignments had been exceeded out randomly or if human beings were requested to volunteer their personal strengths.

Establish Guidelines Right Away to Save Time Later

AT THE VERY BEGINNING OF a collection task, establish fashion and format tips for each member to observe. Putting contributions together from particular people would possibly sound like a clean project that may be sorted at the stop, however often it's no longer smooth in any respect and may be time-consuming. Distribute an e mail or paper containing the font kind and font size of text, headlines, and sub-headlines; margins on all aspects; and what kind of exhibits need to be used. (Better yet, distribute a template with all the favored settings covered.) Keep your organization's formatting regular at the start and you'll be a good deal a lot much less confused and rushed on the last date.

Project Management Gets Results

CONSIDER USING A PROJECT MANAGER for a hard and fast venture, especially in case you're on a large group. If you have got sufficient team humans, you can moreover assign the activity of editor/collator. In a small agency, the challenge supervisor can do the enhancing and collating as properly.

If a task manager isn't used, you run the hazard of all of the man or woman quantities now not flowing in the end. Setting recommendations is a first-rate idea, however it's now not enough on its personal.

One warning is that institution people can emerge as jealous of the venture supervisor early on, because the mission manager gained't have nearly as a good buy art work to do inside the starting of the term. However, this character often finally ends up spending extra hours than another crew member on the venture, and maximum of those hours come at the very surrender of the term, regularly at the cost of sleep. If you really need manage of a mission, project manager is a notable position for you, but definitely be equipped for the strain and past due nights it will probable entail. The greater a collection can damage each company member's assignments down into shorter quantities with common remaining dates, the better off the assignment supervisor might be, because any surprises at the forestall will at least be attainable.

Get Goals Out Into the Open

AT YOUR FIRST TEAM MEETING, have each group member communicate approximately the grade he or she would really like to intention for the task. People are generally pretty honest about this problem. If you are capable of choose your very very own institution, and you see crucial discrepancies among individuals, you may although be capable of transfer businesses. If now not, you may at the least find out what you can assume out of each group member.

If you recognize which you're no longer a mainly robust pupil in comparison to the others inside the group, the alternative university college students on your agency will absolutely apprehend it if you're upfront about your strengths and weaknesses. Most university college college students apprehend that every student has a wonderful set of abilties to offer. The important issue is that everyone has some element they may make a contribution, and most group people will pick out each distinct greater on try than output except.

The A-Student's Secret and Not-So-Secret Resources

Take Advantage of Office Hours

PROFESSORS' OFFICE HOURS CAN BE a totally beneficial useful resource, however you wouldn't apprehend it through way of how few college college students have a propensity to reveal up for them. If you absolutely show up to place of work hours, no longer handiest will most professors want to help you, but they'll frequently offer you with recommendations on what will be on the subsequent take a look at. Also, professors can deliver an reason behind topics in a manner higher suitable to man or woman studying in workplace hours than in class.

Listen to what your professors say to do to achieve success in the elegance, and in the occasion that they don't say, virtually ask. Most professors appreciate even as college college students display interest and really need to have a look at, and displaying as an awful lot as place of work hours is an smooth and powerful manner to talk interest. Not pleasant will going to place of work hours probable reason records your elegance substances better, however displaying strive can honestly make a difference in terms of getting the benefit of the doubt on a check or paper.

Cheat on Your Professor

YOUR PROFESSORS ARE NOT YOUR satisfactory property for getting to know a subject. Some professors decided on their career at the manner to educate, a few to do research, and others for the challenge safety. If you want help in a topic, search out the professors who revel in education, regardless of the reality that they don't train your beauty segment! Professors from exclusive elegance sections obtained't have the capacity to tell you what is going to be on a test, however they is probably capable to help you with the underlying requirements.

As extended as they're not overly busy with their non-public college students, professors who are obsessed with a topic will almost continuously be inclined to help. Find a virtually flattering reason to ask for help, along with taking note of a professor's suitable reputation from extraordinary university college students. If asked approximately your professor, stay unbiased and say you concept studying from a brilliant attitude might decorate your know-how.

Learn Everything You Can From Your English Teachers

ONE OF THE MOST IMPORTANT abilities you may pick out out out up for you to set you apart from others is the capacity to put in writing well. Spending as little as one hour with an first-rate English professor who can actually cross over your writing with you and come up with pointers approximately grammar and fashion may be very precious. Going over each paper you've submitted with a professor for an entire location or semester will make an first rate larger distinction. Don't expect any needed corrections on your papers can be made. Many professors don't problem to accurate greater than the maximum apparent errors.

Writing properly is one of the most effective approaches to face out out of your friends in commands, in machine and graduate faculty packages, and in a while, within the strolling world. The books Elements of Style, with the aid of William Strunk and E.B White, and Woe is I, by way of Patricia T. O'Conner, are remarkable references to preserve reachable. The latter is an easy, short examine, and if you can be given as proper with it, virtually quite exciting. Plenty of online sources exist as properly, and they may be discovered without hassle via searching the phrase "grammar."

Question What He Said She Said He Said

GO ONE STEP FURTHER THAN word-of-mouth facts. Why? It's often no longer accurate. If you've ever completed the game "cellphone," in which a tale is passed from one individual to each other severa times and is slightly recognizable on the prevent, you'll recognize why. Talk to university students approximately commands, but take the extra step to look for professor evaluations, online syllabi, and so on.

It regularly only takes one extra small step to transport ahead of others. I've said similar things typically on this e-book, and repeating this idea isn't any twist of destiny.

Not a whole lot can pay off greater than doing even a touch bit extra than what maximum humans are doing, or to expect just a little more creatively than others. If you're inclined to expect more independently and to try topics others aren't doing, you're in all likelihood to be luckily amazed with the outcomes.

Ask the Aces

SEEK OUT STUDENTS WHO DID well inside the schooling you're going to take. These students must have a far higher draw close of what it takes to reap these schooling than the scholars who didn't do properly, and they will probable recognize the pitfalls to avoid higher than the students who didn't do well. Why? The university university college students who did poorly by no means "cracked the code" of the elegance. Find the students who did properly if you want to have the code cracked for you earlier than elegance even starts offevolved.

Chapter 6: Tips That Couldn't Be Forced Into Other Categories

Rise Above Food Fog

DON'T UNDERESTIMATE THE EFFECT OF your food regimen. Does sugar make you burdened for an hour or , but then you definitely definately crash later on? Does starch make you sleepy? If you're doing all your undergraduate paintings during the usual a long time of 18-22 or so, you're probably able to get away with lots in phrases of ingesting poorly and not sleeping a top notch deal, however possibly not as an entire lot as you accept as true with you studied. Cafeterias generally offer pretty awful alternatives in terms of what to eat, but do your top notch. If you're able to eat frequently real substances and lay off the junk, you may discover which you're capable of hobby better and that you feel a bit sharper at the same time as taking assessments.

Avoid Depending on Drugs to Not Have to Depend on Them

FOOD CAN AFFECT PEOPLE TREMENDOUSLY, but it's even more crucial to be very cautious with more potent materials. Don't do anything in advance than a test this is first-rate than what you will do in any other case. If you typically drink one cup of espresso consistent with day, having an extra one is great (no matter the fact that staying off stimulants of any kind might be even better).

Stay current-day collectively together with your research and you received't need to abuse your frame with stimulants to make it through overdue night time time time after past due night time. Be in particular cautious approximately taking something this is to be had in a pill or powder to growth your energy, because of the truth in the long run you may be putting yourself up for a global of problem through the use of tough tablets. Choose rest and a healthful eating regimen that allows you to have a smooth mind and enough strength to get your artwork finished, and also you'll set your self up thoroughly for life after college while your frame won't be pretty as forgiving.

Go to the Front of the Class

IF YOU FEEL UNCOMFORTABLE SITTING the the front and center in elegance, simply sit down in the the the front but off to the component. This tip is going along facet the idea of retaining apart your college schooling consultation of your social existence. You can communicate to friends in a category earlier than or after elegance, however inside the direction of sophistication try and sit down in a gap wherein you may have minimal distractions, typically because of this up the the front. If you're sitting subsequent to a person who continuously dreams to speak to you, and also you feel rude telling that man or woman to forestall, make up an excuse to take a seat a few other location if desired, or just respond tons tons much less and plenty much less until that individual gets the trace.

Students who are plenty much less targeted and who communicate more although have a tendency to sit down inside the lower lower lower back even in college, so the within the direction of the the the front you may sit, the a bargain plenty much less distracted you may be via them. Leave the distractions outside of sophistication hours, and also you'll soak up the fabric hundreds better. As an advantage, at the same time as a professor sees your diploma of consciousness, she or he may be even extra inclined to assist if there may be some factor you're now not pretty grasping.

Control Time

USE TWO ALARM CLOCKS. I can't recollect a much less complex, but more crucial, tip than this one. Your professors (and future employers) aren't probable to without a doubt accept as real with that your alarm clock "didn't go off." They'll recognize you pressed snooze too generally, or set your clock incorrectly, or simply slept thru the alarm. The essential factor, despite the fact that, is that there may be such an smooth and reasonably-priced approach to make sure this doesn't arise that it must be commonplace for absolutely everyone to apply alarm clocks. One of the two clocks may be plugged in, however make sure that at least one of the two is battery-operated so a power outage within the direction of the night time time doesn't reset the clocks.

Choose Not to Snooze

IF YOU CAN, GET within the dependancy of waking up whilst the alarm first jewelry. In special terms, don't use the snooze alarm. Getting up right away is kind of like pulling a bandage off, where short, intense ache can be better than lengthy, drawn-out ache. Pressing snooze usually makes humans enjoy drowsier, but the most important element is that pressing snooze once can too without problem result in urgent it instances... then three times... then 8 instances. Also, as speedy as snooze has been pressed, it's a small step to turning the alarm off completely.

I recognize I'm likely over-exaggerating a bit right here by using basically describing the snooze button due to the reality the "gateway" button, but if you can train yourself to certainly upward thrust up right away at the same time as the number one alarm is going off, it becomes a addiction that becomes much less difficult and less difficult through the years. Getting up whilst your alarm first earrings may even help make sure that you'll rise up in time for work, in which the outcomes of showing up late will in all likelihood rely extra than being late for sophistication.

Manage When Life Gets in the Way of School

ILLNESS, FAMILY PROBLEMS AND different problems rise up on occasion and can cause you to overlook a test or task. Getting in advance on projects can help prevent problems to a degree, however there might be instances even as you're blindsided and it's nearly not feasible to get topics executed or to make it to elegance for a take a look at. In those times, the first step you ought to take is to the touch your professors as speedy as you recognize that you won't be able to do your art work. In times in which the neglected challenge or test need to clearly have an effect on your grade, you'll probable should approach your professors to discover what alternatives you've got, if any, to make up what you neglected.

There are pretty easy matters you may do this may increase your probabilities of being granted a favorable choice—take obligation for lacking the paintings and provide an answer. If you take obligation for missing the paintings, your professors will see you as a accountable person. You're the best who is requesting special remedy, and if there can be any way you can don't forget to make it easier on the professor if you need to make up the art work, make sure which you specific this. If you can examine this lesson properly, you'll be a huge step ahead of maximum of your friends close to the strolling global, wherein bosses appearance a good deal more favorably upon employees who provide potential solutions while imparting troubles.

Choose Enthusiasm and Optimism Over Envy and Cynicism

MAKE A POINT OF AVOIDING green with envy or cynical people, and as an alternative, try to preserve near out with powerful, enthusiastic people. Find supportive buddies, own family, and mentors, and restriction touch with poor humans. Be especially cautious approximately sharing massive plans with bad folks who could in all likelihood try and discourage you.

One important caveat is which you'll want to examine to distinguish among terrible humans and people who want the best for you, however have precious facts to proportion. If you recognize someone who is usually very exquisite and supportive, it's in fact very critical to pay attention to the unusual times at the same time as that character does deliver up an obstacle to go through in mind. Here's an example of the manner this may look:

Student: I'm going to be converting my essential to art work subsequent semester.

Pessimist: Art? Who are you, Picasso now? All that training goes to visit artwork? There's no coins in paintings, everybody is aware of that.

Supporter: Art looks as if a fun fundamental, and also you've constantly had a flair for it. Have you belief about what education want to go together with artwork to make certain you'll be able to manual yourself, together with taking marketing or pc technological expertise commands?

Seek the Uncomfortable Truth

TRY TO GO TO WHERE the answers are, in vicinity of where the answers are most without troubles decided. Many university college students leave out out on locating genuine career records because of the reality they preserve on with speaking to those with whom they may be maximum comfortable. Who are the first rate belongings? People strolling in a particular profession are an great wager, but probably even better are those going into a selected profession whose parents are doing the identical aspect. The son or daughter of a scientific health practitioner will probable not most effective understand approximately what the career is like, however moreover have an amazing experience of the internships to are in search of for out, the classes to take, and research opportunities.

It tremendous takes a little more studies in existence to get lots higher solutions, however you do ought to take the more step. Many human beings are searching out online or ask those closest to them, however the maximum entire solutions are a step or past those techniques. Don't wait to be pushed to try this, because it gained't take place. In fact, "pushing" takes place a good deal much less and lots less as time goes on. Elementary university teachers are generally encouraging, even as only a few excessive university teachers are, fewer university professors are, or even less humans inside the going for walks worldwide are. Learning may be an increasing number of self-directed as your training and existence goes on, and you could in fact get a soar on the opposition at a more youthful age through the usage of being inclined to are searching for out the pleasant data, irrespective of wherein it's discovered.

College: The Big Transition

Interview Your Roommate

IF YOU PLAN ON LIVING in a dorm freshman yr, call or e mail your assigned roommate in advance than university starts offevolved. If it's obvious the character isn't an fantastic healthy for you as a roommate, try to switch your residing preparations as brief as feasible, as it's generally plenty much less complicated to make this variation early on in the school three hundred and sixty five days.

If you're worried approximately offending the individual, apprehend that he or she is likely to find out you absolutely as incompatible. You don't should live with a person just like you, but you will need a roommate with behavior you may tolerate. For instance, if you need quiet and going to sleep early, and your roommate prefers gambling track for your dorm room till three:00 am, it's in all likelihood now not going to be genuine for you or your grades.

Do Some Registration Reconnaissance

A LITTLE RESEARCH BEFORE REGISTERING for training may additionally need to make all the distinction in the worldwide. Registration commonly takes location in some unspecified time in the future of the middle of every zone or semester, and it could frequently sneak up on you even as you're genuinely busy. The notable time to do research on commands and professors is at the start of every vicinity or semester whilst your artwork load is reasonably slight and you may without issue discover which of your friends are taking particular classes. If you write down their preliminary thoughts on instructions and professors, all you may need to do in a while is double-check this data right earlier than registration. Even in case you don't go beyond finding out their initial thoughts, you'll though have plenty greater knowledge than maximum college college college students. After all, the virtually awful professors regularly make themselves recognised right away!

Consider the use of Microsoft Excel or a web software to music information on education and professors. Being able to type statistics resultseasily and in masses of 1-of-a-type processes can be a completely effective tool. You may additionally even want to maintain in mind strolling in this spreadsheet with severa specific university college students who've comparable dreams as a manner to growth its effectiveness. You can function the important information-keeper even as they accumulate the facts for you, or higher however, set up an internet-primarily based software program program or forum that anyone you provide get entry to to can edit.

Create Weekend Options

EARLY ON, TRY TO make pals who don't birthday celebration an excessive amount of so that you should have numerous social options at the weekends. This method becomes very critical if you have some of art work to finish on weekend days. If you may't find out humans to hang around with inside the dorms, hold in thoughts golf equipment or intramurals, in particular those that focus on analyzing or sports activities sports that incorporate waking up early at the weekends. Clubs that need to do with outside sports activities are a top notch example of the latter.

Making buddies with folks who aren't into partying each weekend doesn't imply you want to keep away from activities. What it approach is that on nights when you have hundreds to do tomorrow, your preference gained't be restrained to staying in through yourself or staying out masses later than you desired and probably not feeling so exceptional the subsequent morning.

If you're making non-partying pals early on, you signal to others which you revel in placing out with unique kinds of humans. By maintaining your social options open from the beginning, you could avoid the awkward feeling that you have abandoned some human beings in need of others.

Pick Your Roommates When You Can

BE VERY CAREFUL WHEN CHOOSING roommates as speedy as you have got a preference, usually which means that after your freshman 12 months. Many proper friendships were out of place due to the reality two or more human beings didn't feature well as roommates, and this introduced stress and anxiety can with out problems have an impact on grades. Think not best about you'll want to live with, but additionally who would be the extraordinary roommate. These may be very one-of-a-kind measures! If you spend all your take a look at time outdoor of your dorm/condo/house, your roommates ought to probable rely lots a good deal less, but they though have an impact for your standard strain tiers (and sleep time). You can usually find sports or pass maintain out on the "fun" houses, but understanding you have got were given got a predictably quiet region to sleep can absolutely help restriction pressure and increase your strength at some point of the day.

Chapter 7: Skip Class Sparingly

COLLEGE IS THE FIRST TIME maximum university college students are away from domestic for a respectable time frame. I can guarantee that you could see a sizable variety of techniques nicely this is treated! You'll see university college students who had been shy in excessive university determine to break out in their shells and be outgoing. You'll see college students who were given in trouble loads in immoderate college all at once mature and no longer go out until they finish their homework. These are the first-class modifications. You're moreover assured to appearance many university college students who can't cope with having a lot freedom unexpectedly, and those university students regularly slip fast. Although it's regularly things like alcohol or exclusive tablets which can be the deliver of the issues, what commonly receives them in trouble in terms of school is skipping instructions.

Try to constantly go to elegance besides there's a without a doubt well motive not to move (in preference to satisfactory going if there's a exceptional cause to transport). Consistently attending commands is in particular crucial the first 12 months or , because of the truth you can without a doubt get in problem via manner of skipping commands early on and making it a dependancy. Generally, simplest the toughest schooling can nevertheless be failed if a student attends each elegance, but any beauty can be failed if sufficient training are not noted. After a while, you may determine out which instructions you may pass proper proper right here and there, and you'll possibly even make higher use of the magnificence time you skipped. In stylish, although, the simplest way to stay on the right tune is to clearly visit each elegance until you're sick or there's a real emergency.

Create Calm, Even When Surrounded by using using way of Chaos

TRY EARPLUGS. IT'S AMAZING absolutely how a first-rate deal sound the coolest ones block out. You may also moreover have to try some top notch sorts of earplugs to find those who work top notch for you. They'll possibly in no way feel certainly comfortable, but the benefits will probably outweigh any pain. Introverts might understand earplugs even extra than extraverts, as introverts have a tendency to get distracted extra with out hassle, but even extraverts need quiet take a look at time from time to time.

Earplugs additionally can be very useful with reference to sound asleep, especially inside the dorms. Strategies collectively with the usage of earplugs to gain extra manipulate over your environment may be very beneficial, as they rely on your non-public movements in place of on you trying to alternate the actions of others.

Outline Your Path and Work Backwards

LIST THE CLASSES YOU WILL (or may probably) need to take to satisfy your diploma requirements together with the overall education commands that hobby you the most. The in advance you may create this listing, the higher off you'll be, as you could accumulate notes on the ones education and their corresponding professors alongside the manner. Also, with the beneficial aid of expertise which training you need to take early on, it will probably be plenty less hard for you to plot beforehand for commands which is probably first-class furnished as quickly as in line with year as an opportunity of every quarter or semester.

Your listing of desired schooling need to be with out problem available to you so you can input notes whenever you look at new records. The thriller proper right here is that the quantity of more artwork to collect this data is in reality very small, however the payoff may be very massive! (You'll word that the preceding sentence simply is probably the state of affairs of this e-book.)

Chapter 8: Major Ideas

Don't Get Weeded Out

MOST MAJORS TEND TO HAVE one or "searching down" commands that arise early on, however the reality that schools received't constantly admit such commands exist. The purpose of those instructions is to appearance whether or now not or not students are absolutely lessen out for a specific most critical. A common mistake is for students to count on commands in a primary will get an increasing number of tough. The truth is that looking down instructions are frequently the maximum difficult in a exquisite, so in case you really need to stay in a particular most important, don't get too discouraged via a tough elegance early on.

The critical factor is to discover which commands interior a selected primary are known as the eliminating commands. Word on those training frequently receives out fast, so college college students who commenced out collectively with you may already recognize which ones they are. If not, the tremendous deliver is likely to be older university university college students in your precise critical. These students have to probable be professors' assistants in a number of your instructions. The subsequent possibility might be to test with an manual internal your most important.

Once you recognize which elegance serves the cause of disposing of the weaker or an awful lot a good deal less critical college college students, you may placed it in angle. You'll recognize that you'll in all likelihood need to art work pretty a chunk tougher to get a very good grade in that elegance, but you'll moreover apprehend that terrible performance doesn't always mean you'll do poorly in that particular principal or which you need to trade majors. If you don't select out the getting rid of education, you would possibly mistakenly assume that all the instructions may be that hard.

Try Potential Majors Early

SWITCHING MAJORS AT LEAST ONCE, if now not numerous instances, appears to be a university life-style. The secret's to start this technique as early on as viable. One desirable manner to check out majors is to take training that fulfill every a popular training requirement and a call for for the primary you need to evaluate. This technique ensures you're no longer wasting any commands, as all the instructions recall toward your selected requirements.

Since tremendous education training are decrease-diploma, some specific way to check out capability majors is to sit down in on some higher-degree courses in every essential that interests you. Most professors can be glad to will let you sit down in on a category or , and if the splendor is big sufficient, you might be able to simply walk in and sit down down down without asking. By checking out the better-diploma publications, you'll get a far better revel in of what's expected of college college students and the problem diploma of the vital.

Do a few research early immediately to keep away from spending an additional year or extra in university due to the fact you switched your primary overdue in the game. Changing your thoughts approximately your number one ten instances at the same time as you're despite the fact that doing all your fashionable education art work is a lot much less luxurious in phrases of time and money than changing it sincerely as quickly as once you've completed maximum of the art work in a primary you now not need.

Keep an Eye at the Future

WHY ARE YOU IN COLLEGE? Are you planning on going to graduate university? If so, is it the grades in your important or your usual grades that depend wide variety range? How you will be evaluated is essential to find out, as it could certainly have an effect on wherein you have to direct your efforts. For example, permit's say which you need to enter a topic wherein graduate schools commonly have a look at your fundamental GPA. In this situation, it might be without a doubt worth it to install greater time on a hard number one elegance although it manner you slip a bit in a couple of modern-day education guides. On the opposite hand, if certainly it's your common GPA that topics most, you won't need to waste all your time on one number one elegance with a view to get bumped up a half of of-grade if it method dropping down a 1/2-grade or extra in or 3 different training!

If it's a difference amongst passing or failing a hard elegance, that's a exquisite tale, however definitely be aware about how lots time you're spending on each beauty and what you count on to be possible in phrases of grades. Overall GPA and a delegated critical have a tendency to be the most critical elements for masses graduate packages, but now not typically, so do a bit of research to look what graduate colleges are seeking out so that you can plan a while for that reason.

Ask Yourself What Comes Up Over and Over for You

PAY ATTENTION TO YOUR LONG-TERM feelings and goals. If you've continuously wanted to be a medical doctor, don't permit one beauty deter you. You may also moreover additionally revel in instances whilst a tough elegance or vicinity will make you need to alternate to an much less complex essential, however do your incredible to stick with a few factor will circulate you inside the route of your career desires. You can get a pastime in a exercising department with a biology degree, but you're no longer probably to get a interest in technological knowledge with a amusement studies diploma!

The rewards of a specific important commonly have a tendency to come lower back lower again beyond because of your schooling, not early, so it's essential to live with the important you really need. Besides the casting off training, other early training may not notable be hard, but they'll additionally in all likelihood be elegant and probably even dull. The higher-degree instructions will be inclined to be the profitable and interesting ones. Plus, the genuine reward comes at graduation time, at the identical time as you could proudly look again on sticking with a tough principal that gadgets you up for an high-quality career or graduate school.

Major for Work, Minor for Fun or for Insurance

TRY TO USE YOUR MAJOR to prepare for a career, as that is the main thing of going to college. If you receive as proper with you studied schooling in a particular primary are thrilling, however you're no longer positive what type of art work they might bring about, take into account the usage of a minor or electives to take the ones training. A minor can frequently be sufficient to qualify for art work in a specific location, however although it isn't, you can usually take greater instructions later as a 2nd main at some point of your undergrad years or perhaps after you graduate. Being able to name unique commands you took in a sure maximum critical in your resume can offer a boost in your credentials.

There are lots upon hundreds of former university university students who remorse getting a "vain" diploma in a easy fundamental they decided on as it modified into easy, or exciting, or a person informed them that every one that mattered became getting a degree, irrespective of important. Don't recall this lie! Yes, getting a degree is treasured in evaluation to now not getting a degree, and loads of corporations gained't rent for sure positions until the applicant has a bachelor's degree.

When you are starting out to your profession and function very little experience, your diploma serves as an opportunity for experience. After some years of real-international experience, the primary received't depend as a whole lot anymore, however at the start it may absolutely make a difference.

Build Your GPA with Forgettable Classes

GETTING INTO GRADUATE SCHOOL TYPICALLY is composed in particular of topics: 1) grades and more than one) standardized take a look at scores. Even despite the fact that I said in advance that a few graduate faculties care more approximately typical GPA and a few about foremost GPA, be cautious of absolutely focusing for your grades to your most vital, because you'll in all likelihood end up looking to visit graduate university for some element particular than you in the beginning expected.

A very powerful way to build up your time-honored GPA is to trying to find out the very first-rate widespread schooling commands. Students have a tendency to talk about the ones lessons quite a chunk, so that they're usually no longer too tough to find out. If you're unsure of your number one, you'll need to weigh taking clean elegant education schooling with taking fashionable schooling education to check out numerous majors. If you're useless-set on one fundamental, even though, and apprehend precisely what you need to do with it, preserve your focus with the aid of manner of taking the proper famous education commands so you can placed it slow and strength into the commands that simply be counted range to you while constructing a stable foundation to your easy GPA.

Pave the Road to Your Future with Internships

DEPENDING ON YOUR MAJOR, one of the maximum important steps inside the route of locating a undertaking once you graduate is to get superb internships during one or extra summers. Ask older students in your important how internships art work to your situation, or higher however, ask an consultant. Internships are often omitted with the aid of many college college students, but they look outstanding on resumes. Also, the earlier internships may be done, the higher, as they may offer you with a experience of what art work in a subject is simply like. You'll get a feel of the profession track, the amount of hours humans paintings, the get dressed code, and perhaps even earnings statistics. Internships are a first rate way to get the enjoy companies want, imparting you with a bonus when you graduate.

Chapter 9: Things You Will Realize After College That You Can Learn Now Instead

Charge Ahead to Open Doors

IT OFTEN WORKS BETTER TO plan for a few element precise and exchange your thoughts than to "hold your options open." When you are moving closer to some thing, it's simpler to decide out what you do and don't like. It might also appear paradoxical, however doors first-class typically will be inclined to open even as we're moving in the path of a goal, in spite of the truth that it seems the possibilities are for a few thing tangential or perhaps definitely unrelated.

When you try to figure out everything to your head, there can be answers that you are missing. Also, while you count on that a few thing isn't possible, you'll will be inclined to locate solutions that make stronger this horrible belief. When you think alternatively about what you want, and decide to discern out how the ones goals will be viable to accumulate, that's whilst doors can open for you. Decide what you need, and then draw upon the belongings and statistics of others. You can also find your alternatives are lots more expansive than you formerly concept.

Follow Dreams or Money or Both. Just Try to Get at Least One!

SOME BOOKS AND PEOPLE ADVISE college university students to "follow their goals," whilst others recommend to go into something career makes the most cash on the manner to have the resources to enjoy lifestyles out of doors of labor. Both arguments have their merits, but the vital thing isn't always to go into artwork you don't like for low pay! Often students genuinely have handiest a indistinct sense of what severa jobs pay, but it's well worth it to make the effort to investigate this early on in university.

If you could flow right right into a location you want, one huge gain is that you'll be much more likely to stay with it and positioned in the time and effort to honestly do properly. Being in a position to take care of your self financially is very important, but paintings takes up an entire lot of the day that you really need to make certain you acquired't be miserable in a positive career.

If you're uncertain of what you need to do, there are a couple of various paths you can take, of which I may endorse. First of all, if you have narrowed your alternatives down to two or 3 fields, begin with the only that hobbies you maximum, and move after it with everything you've got. Only thru virtually going after a few element are we able to research what it may provide. The one-of-a-kind possible course, if a excessive-paying role is feasible for you, is to try to make and shop as a outstanding deal coins as feasible for some years. A excessive-paying venture will provide the cash you want to both flow decrease returned to school or to in any other case attempt severa careers while not having to be as involved about money for some time.

Treat College Like the Cafeteria of Activities It Is

YOU WILL NEVER HAVE BETTER possibilities to try out such a whole lot of one-of-a-type sports so with out issue and rate correctly as within the course of your university years. During the university year, those possibilities can range from out of doors activities to net hosting radio suggests to intramural sports sports. College clubs frequently require very little, if any, dedication, so you can strive setting out with loads of them to look what works for you. Many membership- or college-sponsored sports activities are subsidized, so take advantage of them.

Summers may be times for paid or unpaid internships, residing in some other location cheaply, or tour. You aren't in all likelihood to have studies after university while your costs, which includes hire, can be so low. In truth, many university students will stay at home inside the course of the summer time and now not pay lease. Be positive that is the first-rate desire for you, as there are regularly better opportunities and further attractive options for growth with the resource of going faraway from home for one or extra summers. Look into what's available, and make the maximum of this opportunity-filled time of your life!

Take Advantage of Great Exchange Rates

SOME OF THE MOST AMAZING offers during university are the exchange packages, wherein trying out a super school inside the same usa, or maybe each different america of america, doesn't price masses extra than a regular region or semester at your current faculty! The applications are commonly established to encompass tour and hotels, the latter of that could particularly be a undertaking to find out to your non-public.

Don't underestimate the charge of home change applications. Domestic applications are in large part unnoticed in need of the global applications, as going to each other u . S . Is such an interesting opportunity and regularly the kind of fantastic deal, however domestic applications offer advantages as properly. For instance, you may strive out residing in a special part of the united states, in any other case you might be able to do an undergraduate change application at a college that has a graduate software in which you have interest. The latter preference might be a exquisite manner to reveal your hobby inside the school and to make certain it might be the splendid choice for you.

The worldwide programs are often unbelievably right offers, and allow for delivered journey at some stage in breaks or earlier than or after this machine. Also, the commands which can be provided are normally clean relative to training at domestic, allowing university college students the time and power to find out on their personal.

Appreciate Your Peers

ONE OF THE BIGGEST CHANGES after university is that you will no longer be spherical a fixed this is so close in age and has such bendy schedules. Keep this in thoughts and make the maximum of your social alternatives in the route of a while in college. Making friends may also moreover get more difficult as years flow on, and having a brilliant center employer of buddies from college may additionally need to make the transition into the walking worldwide less complicated and extra amusing, especially if some of them skip to the equal area as you after graduation. College is possibly the final time of your lifestyles at the same time as you'll be around hundreds of different human beings to your age group each day, and that's no longer a few element to be taken as a right!

In truth, every so often I wonder what number of graduate college candidates want to transport once more to highschool simply to get lower lower back even a bit of that enjoy.

Enjoy the Anticipation of Coming Home

IF YOU GO AWAY TO a four-yr college proper after high college, there's a in reality fine benefit on the identical time because it comes time for holidays. You won't surely get this element until you've each professional and out of place it, however coming domestic from university and seeing all of your vintage friends is a incredible feeling. Something about the mixture of beginning an exciting new lifestyles and having a lot to speak about combined with a bit homesickness can draw antique buddies closer.

The breaks you'll get at Thanksgiving are frequently mainly sweet, as maximum human beings commonly pleasant have own family duties on that Thursday night, and masses of humans are available to loaf around on Friday and Saturday (and now and again even Wednesday). If you need to appearance humans you went to high school with, head out on the Friday and Saturday night time after Thanksgiving.

There's no time just like the college years and possibly a 3 hundred and sixty 5 days or two after to appearance all your antique friends on the local bars and different hangouts. Take advantage of this, as it obtained't closing. People will circulate away, get married, have youngsters, in any other case scatter, and become more tough to supply collectively. Appreciate the ones years as they appear further to taking pictures and movies of the extraordinary times, and you'll have reminiscences to last an entire existence.

Discover the Truth About Teamwork

WHILE IT IS IMPORTANT TO learn how to artwork with others, possibilities are that the significance of teamwork is probably hyped up in college and the importance of unbiased art work will be underestimated. Working successfully with others is honestly critical, however it's additionally very important so one can get paintings completed independently. Companies frequently stress the significance of teamwork, but what is generally supposed is the functionality to get alongside side others. The most common state of affairs is for organizations to return together in a meeting, and then for people to move off to complete the work on their very personal. Be capable to speak that you may artwork properly every on teams and with the useful resource of the use of your self while you do hobby interviews, and if you can lower lower back this up, your employers is probably happy to have hired you.

Find Work Opportunities Designed for New Grads

SOME TRUTH EXISTS IN THE oft-repeated lament, "I can't get a assignment with out revel in, but I can't get revel in with out a method." Internships are probably the nice treatment for this, however another answer is to search for agencies that actively trying to find out graduating college university students for control or wonderful schooling packages. Management consulting organizations are a extraordinary instance of this.

Companies are interested by graduating college students for a mixture of factors. For one element, new graduates are seen as much less tough to teach by way of way of a few groups, as the scholars haven't however evolved entrenched mind approximately how topics have to be executed. Second, college graduates will be predisposed to have a number of energy and are frequently willing to pay dues with grunt paintings, lengthy hours, and relatively low pay. Lastly, and especially key for consulting organizations, younger graduates will be inclined to not however have households and are therefore extra amenable to adventure and relocation.

Your college's career center must have a extremely good experience of the businesses looking for college university students to hire right out of university, as those are possibly to be the organizations the career middle is in touch with for profession festivals and internships. Seek out those companies and jobs, and you can set yourself up for a high-quality profession route, probably even placing your self rapid in advance of others who have greater revel in.

Chapter 10: Making The Most Of Lectures

Being Prepared for Success

Lectures are an important a part of many publications if you want to be successful. Therefore it's far vital to be prepared for lectures to take full gain of them. Preparation comes in lots of paperwork, and the extra prepared you're, the extra capable you'll be of absorbing important records from the lecture. This can also serve you very well in exams or midterms, and could most possibly be even more beneficial for the examination.

One a part of being prepared for lectures is having a tremendous idea of the content cloth fabric. Course outlines typically provide the project rely range, large idea, or scenario be counted for each lecture or week. Getting statistics facts earlier than the lecture can be very beneficial for succeeding. This will help you perceive key elements which can be discussed in the lecture. Furthermore, you'll be much more likely to procedure what is being taught efficaciously if you understand what's being mentioned in popular.

Another portion of being prepared to make the maximum of your lectures is reading about the hassle ahead. It may be very commonplace to have assigned readings for a route, and due to the reality you have to study the ones besides, why no longer take a look at in advance so that you have a organization draw near of the cloth. If the readings are not assigned without delay, you may however have a look at chapters of the textbook which might be related to the concern within the direction define. A number one gain to studying earlier than the lecture is that you may understand what ideas you're having trouble with, and because of this pays extra hobby to them within the lecture. If you continue to do no longer recognize, you will be able to ask the professor proper away, in place of delaying and likely forgetting about it.

In addition, it is vital to be organized to your lectures bodily. Having the proper equipment, which includes your writing utensils and pocket e book, will help ensure that you may be privy to vital elements. In addition, it's far crucial to be inside the proper united states of mind even as attending lectures. Make positive to fulfil your number one dreams fulfilled, at the side of starvation, thirst and bladder, as having any urge within the path of the lecture will motive you to lose popularity. Sleep has a tendency to be the need frequently neglected or lessen once more on, it truly is a risky compromise to make, you revel in to be refreshed to be at your top regular universal overall performance.

By being organized, you are placing yourself in a terrific role so you can take advantage of lectures. You may be able to ask accurate questions, take nicely notes and stay centered, all helping your success.

Using the Tools at Your Disposal

It is always beneficial to apply as maximum of the tool at your disposal as you may to finish impact. Lectures, tutorials, labs and seminars are in all likelihood a number of the most effective gear provided in education, so the use of them nicely will circulate a protracted manner in supporting you prevail.

If you arrived at lectures organized, you're already properly-set, so do not allow this opportunity go to waste. Paying hobby in lectures is essential. As a quit result, you need to keep away from any capability distractions. This consists of turning off (or on the minimum silencing) things like your mobile phone, and closing tabs to your laptop on the manner to distract you. In addition, even as it may be amusing sitting on the aspect of your pals if that hinders your capacity to reputation, it's miles a first rate idea to keep socialization and lectures separate. It is a top notch concept to avoid distractions in lectures so you can supply your undivided hobby to the more crucial challenge handy.

Having pinnacle lecture notes will assist you prepare for tests, midterms and assessments. As a stop result, you need to take the high-quality notes you could at some point of splendor. It can be tempting to install writing the whole lot the professor says or as little as feasible, however every strategies aren't perfect. Writing an excessive amount of will bury vital elements under other subjects that aren't as useful. Writing too little can also purpose you to miss those elements. In addition, both will make analyzing extra hard, the former presenting you with an excessive amount of to take a look at, on the identical time as the latter will now not offer you with enough. This makes it crucial to have right notes, as you need to have the ability to make use of them as a outstanding take a look at device.

There has a tendency to be lots of supportive analyzing corporations to be had to assist with instructors (and probable for special matters too), in general with out fee. Such assets are underutilized with the beneficial useful resource of most college students, which makes them even higher for the ones seeking out greater help or recommendation. It is probably that you may be capable of get plenty of time one-on-one with a helper, and may studies higher strategies of fixing issues, or one-of-a-kind strategies to help you in the course. As a result, resource businesses are a remarkable aid that ought to not be omitted.

Like help organizations, place of business hours with the professor or TA are each different beneficial resource that is not carried out completely via maximum university college students. One professor knowledgeable us his thumbs would possibly get sore due to the reality he is probably twiddling them for a while at the equal time as searching earlier to university college students to wait his place of job hours. Attending place of job hours will permit you to end up extra familiar with the teacher, and vice versa. For legal reasons, we will neither affirm nor deny whether or no longer or now not professors admit to being greater beneficiant whilst marking college students whom they understand. In addition, even in case you do not have any questions in thoughts, you will likely studies from the solutions to distinct scholar's questions, and the present day views would possibly likely even increase questions you in no way idea of earlier than. This technique that you could kill multiple birds with one stone via attending administrative center hours.

An expert in any area makes use of machine to their maximum capability. Likewise, the usage of powerful sources given to you to similarly your expertise will assist placed you on target to fulfillment. So, it's miles useful to take entire gain of have a observe notes, help companies and administrative center hours, at the identical time as they will be to be had to you.

Putting Together What You Have Learned

During any semester, you'll be anticipated to have a look at loads, and frequently the entirety have to ultimately come collectively. However, with excessive requirements, you can't simply preference that everything may be all proper, you have to placed an attempt to make certain it does. Hence, it's miles vital to consolidate your learning regularly just so you will be well-organized for any assessments, which include the final examination.

To be able to located the puzzle together, you need all of the pieces. This is why it's far crucial to keep a organization draw close of all content material brought for the duration of the direction. After each lecture, you want to make certain which you have met the gaining knowledge of goals. If you haven't, it turns into even more essential to study what have become protected. It is an lousy lot less complicated to cope with one getting to know motive that you may have not noted at the stop of the day, as compared to many studying desires disregarded clearly earlier than an assessment. This way that keeping all the pieces on your course puzzle intact will help make big strides inside the route of being capable of placed it collectively in some time.

Ideally, puzzle portions might not decay significantly over time, however, any competencies or ideas determined out simply can if now not used continuously. Thus, it's miles essential to keep stay on pinnacle of them in some unspecified time in the future of the semester, so that you will not be struggling to recollect subjects decided out early on inside the course of an assessment. Keeping on top of things on all vital topics discovered out within the semester will suggest that in area of relearning, you will be capable of spend more time on reviewing, as a way to be an asset for checks, midterms and checks.

Finally, as quickly as you have have been given all of the portions gift and in pristine circumstance, setting all of it collectively isn't always as tons of a mission. To assist stimulate the way, you should try and examine questions that contain many concepts together. Exam evaluate questions have a tendency to do this, similarly to questions for very last evaluation within the textbook. With this workout, it will be masses simpler to prepare a stable answer in a number one evaluation.

Help! My Lectures Don't Help: Independent Study

In lifestyles, you could every now and then want to learn how to do subjects in your very own. This applies in training too, analyzing is your obligation, in particular in university and university. It is the professor's hobby to try and train what is anticipated to be trained, however once in a while that isn't always sufficient. As a surrender end end result, in case you feel you are not learning enough, you could constantly do it yourself.

Self-studying will become a bargain less complicated even as you apprehend what you want to analyze. As mentioned earlier than, you may generally discover this inside the path define, and if no longer, you still have your textbook as a guide. You can set your agenda at the same time as self-studying, and this could be beneficial to assist stay at the right music. Once you comprehend precisely what you want to research, it is a lot less hard to transport on and examine what's required.

The direction textbook is a extraordinary area to begin analyzing with the useful resource of using yourself. Courses are normally based definitely totally on textbooks, and intently related. In addition, textbooks commonly feature in-intensity reasons, in a extra formal revel in than lectures. Furthermore, self-exams and workout questions in textbooks will assist you make certain which you are information the mind which you are analyzing. Due to textbooks being related to the route, and having equipment so one can will let you see how you're doing, they make a exquisite stepping stone on the path of self-reading.

Other than the direction textbook, there can be maximum in all likelihood an array of related records to be had at your library. Going past the scope of the textbook or route could make your expertise even deeper, and as a result you'll be properly prepared for extension questions designed to split the not unusual college college students from the first rate ones. However, be cautious even as going past, as you do no longer want to take too much time a long way from matters nicely absolutely worth more marks within the route. Despite this, it's far but a high-quality idea to go to your library to assist in addition your expertise thru books that move greater in-intensity than your textbook.

There is each exclusive beneficial useful resource, which can be very big, in which you can also further your know-how for a direction, the Internet. While it's far an awesome beneficial aid, you need to be very cautious. It is easy to get distracted, move too some distance in-intensity, examine subjects explicitly excluded from the direction, and even get wrong statistics, whilst the use of the Internet. Thus, it is crucial to be vigilant while turning to the Internet, although it does offer clean get right of access to to lots of statistics.

On a totally last examine for self-reading, even because it let you loads in records the content material fabric, do not forget about lectures. Even inside the event that they enjoy useless, assessments may have additives simplest noted in lectures, and you cannot come up with the money for to sacrifice this type of a part of your mark. As a stop result, use self-reading as a complement, not a substitute.

Chapter 11: Staying On Track

Avoiding Procrastination like a Pro

A critical barrier in the road, an abyss in our direction or some thing else you could decide upon to call it – procrastination – is the bane of our life for plenty human beings, and a trouble that allows masses human beings to stay stuck or sense out of place on our adventure to fulfillment. The unfortunate part of all of this is that severa us do not realise we are procrastinating. Procrastination is many things, however usually, it tends to be the concept or idea we supply ourselves to take away or waft a assignment to a miles much less vital spot in our thoughts.

It permits you and I like, to make the choice that we are going to have time to finish the mission later, and that we're able to spend time playing video video games, spending it with buddies or a mountain of other motives. The worst detail is on occasion we put off the ones obligations see you later that we both say "Well it's too overdue, I can't get it completed now" or we throw collectively some thing this is so horribly written or incomplete which you recognize your grade is going to go through.

We've executed our research, and we're pretty assured that during case you inform yourself any of the subsequent excuses, you are a sufferer of your procrastination and it wants to be regular!:

1.Waiting for the quality second to finish the venture "Oh, I don't have enough time, I don't have my preferred pencil" and so forth.

2.Telling your self you are much more likely to finish the mission when you're left with a small time frame, or the mission is brief sufficient for a final-minute "21-page History essay? That's do-capable in 2 hours I'd say"

three.Productive procrastination is likewise a factor, wherein you complete or practices other matters in desire to what you have to be prioritizing "I'm going to exercise some piano...for an hour then do my assignment"

four. A commonplace fallacy that professors detest is "I'll be higher prepared later". Professors strategically coordinate lectures, readings, and assignments, so that you need to begin it as soon as it is available, even if you experience underprepared this is in all likelihood intentional on the professor's thing, for it will improve your know-how.

Now you're privy to the manner to perceive the trouble we will bypass immediately to how we will recuperation the problem. It's a clean and candy answer, electricity of mind is right at the same time as tackling procrastination. First, constantly remind yourself that there's maximum probably constantly some issue for you to complete or finish. So, no extra giving your self the excuse of no longer remembering an challenge, or telling your self it's smooth that you may do it later, that's incorrect.

Once you remind yourself – you want to do it. Next, remove all tempting options to completing your work. This includes but isn't always confined to setting out with pals, listening to track and not doing work, watching a movie or TV show where via the give up you've completed a pleasing five% of the undertaking, and whatever else of this variation.

This works due to the truth now there's high-quality one hassle to be able to do, and that's the mission on hand. Finally, you may use strategic techniques in competition to yourself. You can provide yourself an cheaper reward like a snack and smash time gambling video games or placing out. You can deliver yourself a effect if you do now not whole the undertaking, together with reading a further hour. Or you may even make your purpose to not procrastinate regarded to pals and circle of relatives, in case you need to hold to remind you to live on the mission available in preference to watching that movie or going to the park. Follow the above and you'd have conquer a large hurdle that lots people face procrastination.

Studying With or Without Friends

Now comes the awesome debate plenty oldsters have while the time includes have a observe for a quiz, test, examination or a few component else, "Should I even have a observe with _____?" Many folks have friends who might be remarkable at the issue you are suffering in and function mastered the content material cloth you oh-so desire to be definitely as high-quality in. But, simply due to the fact your friend is amazing with the material does not advocate you may be after reading with them. You can be asking us why? Read beneath and ask your self, and count on on it –be sincere.

There's a distinction amongst questioning you recognize the content and knowledge the content material cloth cloth. You may be asking us how that is feasible to trick yourself into this. However, it often occurs while you're analyzing with buddies! How commonly has it passed off, in which you're caught on a hassle or question and in reality cannot determine out the solution, then you definitely definately preserve to invite a chum to finish the problem. As they complete the problem you inform your self which you understood a hundred% of what they did, and you made minor errors and that is why you could not do it. But then you definitely definately keep and do not do the problem your self, imparting you with the fake revel in which you understand the content cloth whilst you don't. This trouble is with out problem solvable.

It is sincerely perfect to take a look at and ask your buddies to study more than one exercise questions with you. However after that is completed, with out searching at what they've finished the least bit, do the query once more by using the usage of your self. It's easy if you can't whole the question perfectly with out concerning your buddy's art work or asking a question you do not understand the idea. However, in case you do complete it well without help or concerning the solution live cautious! Temporary memorization of a way or idea to reply a question isn't always useful in case you forget about about it by the time you want it for a check or examination.

So, the following day or perhaps 2 days from even as you and your buddy do it (Just endure in mind!) flow into lower back to the query and do it another time a few instances. If you can do it flawlessly another time – high-quality! You've probably conquered the bottom idea for that query (Not always the whole location you're having hassle with). And if not. Exercise it once more, assessment beyond techniques and repeat the way to assure yourself you have got observed out it.

Otherwise, do no longer get sidetracked thru analyzing with buddies! You may check with them and do tough questions but it's miles pretty smooth to get distracted or discover yourself off-tune. A awesome manner to stay on situation count if you are reading by myself or with a friend goes to the library, it has an inclination to be a place wherein you and your pals are an entire lot less likely to start gambling around.

Utilizing what's Available to You

Students regularly finish that they will be all on their personal, truly them and the textbook is all this is to be had for them to make use of to preserve their grades. This is a commonplace false impression, and we are able to provide an reason in the back of how you can make use of what's to be had to benefit stellar grades- even in case you're blind to what is to be had -we're capable to expose you a manner to find out what's!

The first and essential most on hand beneficial useful aid to you we've already said, which simply takes place to be your textbook. Your textbook for the path can both be a lifesaver or it can virtually be vain relying for your direction. We're going to count on first that it's miles beneficial.

Your teacher or professor will regularly assign textbook questions, issues and readings which most of the elegance or lecture in no manner even takes a study.

However, here's a little thriller: frequently professors and teachers will pick out questions word-for-word or create a very comparable questions to the readings on quizzes, exams and checks. Not first-class this but the questions and readings give you a plethora of records that you can upload to your skillset for conquering the course.

Feeling misplaced with a idea? Ask for assist or observe hassle answers to get a higher preserve near, and then maintain to do the questions within the textbooks. Often textbooks will offer solution manuals or short answers to problems to help higher your know-how. The reading is likewise there for a purpose, analyzing them will assist your query comprehension while writing your exams and exams.

Another big useful useful resource this is frequently underestimated with the beneficial aid of university college college students, from the number one 3 hundred and sixty 5 days as tons as graduating is the use of the lecturers' or professors' workplace hours! These instructional specialists gets a price to assist college university college students for the duration of those administrative center hours, and trust it or not. Many of them turn out to be extensively bored or paintings on something else due to the fact university college students virtually do no longer come. Why? Most likely because of the reality college students sense shy or anticipate the professor will expect a whole lot less of them for no longer records what they taught in class or lecture. That is honestly no longer proper! Many of the top notch college students attend place of job hours, so professors generally remember the attendees a part of the elite alternatively.

You may fit ask your instructor or professor for help, they might offer an motive for thoughts, go through questions with you, assign practice questions, growth on necessities taught, and loads more. Don't overlook about the help of college students, now and again they may even factor you in the proper path of what you ought to be specializing in when you have a check for a test or exam- and that may be a pleasure on your marks.

The same goes to your TA, or schooling assistant if you have one. All the above can be applied to them as well. You may discover operating with or asking your TA less complicated than your professor, they'll be usually best and function a piece of spare time to help you out. Be cautious asking lecture-unique questions, but, as your TA's maximum possibly are unaware of what you did in magnificence for a particular lecture, and it's miles higher to look or maybe e mail your instructor or professor if you have a particular question.

A very last device we want you to utilize is certain; the net. Whilst being a very distracting tool, if used well hundreds of benefits can be extracted from its use. If you're having hassle with a selected concept or trouble-solving technique there may be an array of resources to be had to you. There are web web sites with a purpose to have lists upon lists of films and readings all at your disposal without rate.

If you have got exhausted the textbook of its questions, the net is a tremendous region in which you find out greater examples to apply your newfound know-how. Be cautious of question formatting and variables however, a few schools, instructional journals and global places also can vary in style in assessment to your own home university. So, adapting to or warding off those questions even as you hold close the standards can be a splendid concept.

Extracurriculars and School

Balancing college and an real existence with a first rate social life can seem tough or close to no longer viable for a few people. It's good enough to experience this manner initially, however a stability can be obtained, do no longer be worried!

It's essential to consider that along issue school, you do need to live life and there are many techniques you can get involved with. Being worried will permit your mind to have a while to loosen up and misery. Trying to look at with a very forced or overburdened mind may be absolutely as horrible as not analyzing in any respect. Extracurriculars are an extraordinary manner to fight pressure and do some element a laugh at the equal time as you're at it.

There are severa unique procedures you can get involved and loosen up, it is not confined to at least one thing or every distinctive. You may be part of a membership or numerous clubs for a rely of reality. You also can be part of a sports sports activities group if this is your trouble, or really an intramural membership in case you're not the terrific but nonetheless experience the bodily interest. Joining the fitness center do distress also can be a terrific manner to hold a healthful body and mind for breaks among studying.

While some of these extracurriculars sound like a considerable amount of relaxation and amusement, it's miles important to take a look at: do now not tackle extra than you can balance together together with your college life! The mistake has been made with the aid of lots of college university college students. You is probably inquisitive about severa taken into consideration one in every of a type golf equipment, all of which you're interested by becoming a member of at the identical time as additionally being part of a sports sports sports group. While some human beings can pull this off in a breeze, take into account the way it works out for you. Will you continue to have time to check and whole assigned obligations? If you have got were given were given the slightest doubt for your mind, don't tackle too many.

A majority of the time, studying or finishing assignments can soak up plenty more time than it appears to. You may additionally moreover allocate hours to studying biology for instance, but by the point you recognize and memorize all of the requirements, it can have with out difficulty taken double the time for which have a have a look at length.

Just keep in mind, balance is top to achievement for your educational profession. It's critical to have some time to your self doing assets you revel in to maintain maximum satisfying brain feature on the same time as you examine and do homework. But it's additionally key now not to overload your self with too much strength of mind to extracurriculars leaving you in a squeeze with time left over to have a test.

Juggling You Courseload

Chapter 12: How To Mastermind A Feasible Plan

Now you have got examine via the bulk of what you could utilize to gain that excellent GPA of four.Zero it's miles vital to mastermind a likely plan wherein you will be capable of assure this runs without problems!

Assuring you have got a complicated plan will assist you achieve success. It's like having the building blocks to a Lego set with remarkable the photograph, very tough but potential. However, it has a tendency to end up lots much less complicated if you have the plans or instructions equipped to gain this. When going via this a part of the e-book, you could ought to revisit and set a present day plan for every 3 hundred and sixty 5 days, or semester counting on how your college runs to prepare yourself a streamlined plan.

The first step to putting in a superb plan is calling your self "Where am I?" for every route, lab, and seminar you've got if the ones pertain to you. And we don't suggest in which you are geographically, however extra in a experience of approaches cushty you enjoy together together with your capacity to recognize the fabric going forwards. Sometimes it can take a bit of time for you to test the waters with multiple the number one labs or lectures and that is adequate! But maintain in thoughts falsely assuring yourself that you'll be simply good enough with a topic is one of the plans that may result in catastrophe if no longer actual.

Another concept to take into hobby whilst installing vicinity your plan is a part of what we noted previously. Try and undergo in thoughts the entirety that frequently takes region and located it into your plan. For instance on the educational element:

- 1 hour each unusual day studying/operating closer to Biochemistry

- 2 hours each regular day reading/practicing Physics

- 2 hours each even day analyzing/training Chemistry

- 30 minutes an afternoon reading/training Biomedical Science

- half of-hour an afternoon reading/training Art History

That's the primary a part of the plan we're looking at. Now as mentioned inside the preceding paragraph, let's examine the entirety else we've had been given to don't forget, like club dedication, teams, and so forth.

- 2 hours an afternoon working in the course of Football with the crew

- 1 hour two times in step with week volunteering at the Humane Society

- 1 hour every particular day on the Veterinary club

- 1 hour as soon as in line with week at the Programming club

- half of-hour times in keeping with week going to place of job hours

It won't look like a whole lot however the 2nd a part of the plan indexed above is very skimpy and has a tendency to be barebones for loads college students that need to be lively or enjoy their spare time. Even in case you do no longer – you'll likely spend that factor (and greater!) analyzing, gambling video video games, or a few issue else you enjoy.

After you've got that all down it is now amazing to physical create a timetable (We advocate the use of a spreadsheet software program application on the laptop) and print it out. Remember to attempt to go away yourself masses of space and further time! Life waits for no man or woman, and masses of things upward thrust up and alternate its lifestyles. Do not worry approximately your self. Your plan is not set in stone, it could be fluid and alternate for the higher over the semester or year.

Prioritizing Leads to Perfection

Now that you have an expertise of the manner to create a plan, it is time to talk about how you may optimize it with prioritization. You're likely now asking us "Why didn't you specify this in advance than you advised me to create the plan?". There is a high-quality purpose for this. The majority of factors are in no way created flawlessly at the number one go with the flow, they take many revisions, edits and refinements to get it pleasant. You have your plan or as a minimum concept about it from what you observe formerly. But now one after the other you may optimize it. Doing optimization and making plans in considered certainly one of a kind steps has an inclination to be lots extra powerful for university kids in place of looking to do each at the equal time, that is why.

The device we particular is prioritization. As stated in the preceding phase we hinted at this with the aid of using stating you need to ask yourself in which you are pertaining to your skills in every of your publications for the yr or semester. That allowed you to allocate greater or much less time to analyzing and education for every of your subjects. We furthermore stated that your plan is malleable and permits change.

If you haven't already, move again to section 4.1 and difficult up an estimate of the time allocations you will require for reading, practicing, golf equipment and so on.

Now that you've finished this format what you have got described in the front of you, assuming you've left masses of area for topics that would pop up within the future, time to loosen up, time to hang around with pals and such.

Some human beings might also additionally moreover will permit you to recognize to attention on what you don't understand first after which skip observe what or are suitable with. This is a faux misunderstanding of what you have to be doing, and we'll let you know why.

Let's say there are subjects that you are taking in university. We'll use Music Theory and Art History for instance. Pretend you're splendid, or maybe sincerely k at Art History but you are suffering along with your Music Theory direction. Traditionally you may be knowledgeable to only awareness on or begin studying Music Theory and go away Art History because of the reality you as a minimum apprehend a number of it. When you do this, human beings have a propensity to increase frustration with themselves. Say you've got been caught on understanding or memorizing the scales related to the treble clef. After you've attempted to test Music Theory and then skip immediately to Art History you've left yourself feeling undefeated, unintelligent and exhausted.

Now, if you have a test the easy brief stuff which you're already adequate or tremendous with you can avoid that situation. Completing or analyzing for the publications you're well off with first is a tactic you can use to easy time and leave room for unique guides you're struggling with. It's a highbrow impact- if you experience you apprehend something in a unmarried vicinity, after which begin to have a test the following it united statesthe feeling you have got for fulfillment and determination. However, the other manner spherical you're left feeling pressured out and defeated and people normally tend to resent reading when feeling like this.

So, check the time desk we requested you to put out within the front of you and put together your have a examine and homework very last touch times in step with what you're able to doing quicker first, and slower or have extra trouble with the second one. This pertains just for your lectures, labs and seminars. Don't fear approximately prioritizing your extracurriculars and different subjects. Allow the ones positions in your plan to be dictated by the point they run or can run spherical your studying and homework crowning glory time.

Detailing Underload and Overload

We've mentioned, lengthy gone over and with a piece of success completed your plan now on the road to success for accomplishing a 4.0, or very high GPA. If you're although feeling a piece harassed, or you're wondering that may be a good deal too easy, preserve studying this section. We'll flow into over what's referred to as your direction load, or what number of guides/instructions you're taking right away consistent with time period (be it a semester or a three hundred and sixty five days).

Typically most colleges allow you to have a plus-minus to your direction load. And what is meant thru this, is which you are allowed to take fewer or greater guides than the normal large supplied via the instructional body, or college. For example, on the University of Guelph, all through a modern-day term/semester college students usually take a 2.Five-credit course load, which for this case's sake is a 5-direction load (each direction being zero.Five credit score). Now, college students can drop to two.Zero credit score, or four guides and regardless of the fact that be a entire-time scholar. This is a exceptional concept for university college college students, and probable you if you're though feeling crushed. That's a twenty percentage cut fee in course load, potentially allowing you to have a large majority of time to commit on your fantastic courses. The downside, however, is you may graduate later.

But don't be concerned. When you graduate degree you'll by no means pay attention the query "So how lengthy did it take you to finish your diploma?" but it is able to be guaranteed at the same time as you're seeking to get a foothold inside the mission marketplace that you may be requested "So, what modified into your not unusual GPA?", or they will test your transcript for your time period or traditional GPA.

Back to the example once more, in preference to losing to 2.Zero credit rating, or 4 guides a scholar can flow into into direction overload. This is wherein you're taking extra than the normal 2.Five credit rating score 5 courseloads. Some schools have a restrict to the most, but many do not. This can be very useful for plenty reasons. Maybe you have got failed a course and need to retake it in the end collectively along side your next semester's courses. Maybe you want to attain a minor, double important or speciality designation for your degree or diploma. Maybe you have really determined an area you need or are right at and need to take courses for amusing. All are motives you may want to enter direction overload.

Only overload or underload if required! If you are too stressed or unable to cope with this sort of excessive load, you can undergo in mind underloading your self. Those of you who're satisfied with in which your GPA stands and your potential to deal with extra stay at a regular load and possibly bear in mind overloading in exquisite activities.

Chapter 13: Getting The Grades

A is for Assignments

The weighting of assignments can vary substantially in the course of courses from having no weight in any respect to having a completely sizable weighting, or a few thing in among. However, although there may be no weighting, there might be a purpose the lecturers spent the effort in developing them, possibly to assist put together you for actual assessments. This approach that it's miles important to try to obtain assignments.

Assignments have a propensity to require hundreds of attempt, which means that procrastination can be brutal. Given this, it is an first rate concept to start as soon as viable on an mission. Being finished early has no outcomes while being past due also can additionally have intense effects, as lots as getting 0 on it. In addition, you will have loads of time to invite questions want to you warfare with a few factor on it. Also, falling inside the returned of can purpose a chain, making you stuck similarly at the back of due to the truth you have got got been too busy completing preceding assignments. Therefore, it is outstanding to start early for assignments.

As the semester progresses, you can look at new subjects as a manner to help enhance your undertaking paintings. This is even much more likely in case you commenced the undertaking early. However, due to the fact you had been in advance, because of this you have got time to make changes and therefore enhance your task and be even more likely to earn a excessive grade. If you possibly did now not start early, it nevertheless is a first rate concept to put in force any new pointers you decided, as you have have been given little reason to lose such marks on a few element that come to be taught in magnificence.

Your paintings is likely going to be examined with a close to eye at the same time as being marked, so you need to accomplish that too earlier than submitting. Whether the task is an English essay, or a Computer Science program, checking your art work cautiously will assist prevent silly errors from slipping through in advance than submission. If it's miles viable, proofread and revise after not looking at your paintings for 48 hours, as this may assist you test it without your mind vehicle-correcting your mistakes mentally. A close eye will circulate an prolonged manner in catching mistakes earlier than they will be located through the person marking them.

Doing well on assignments isn't always tough if you placed the attempt in. Not exquisite will getting particular marks on assignments assist your grades but will better put together you for distinctive tests, because the extra practice can be on hand.

Mastering Quizzes, Midterms and Tests

Quizzes, exams, midterm tests, or any mixture of them, make up a massive a part of the final grade in maximum courses. Not simplest that, but marks also are frequently easier to return lower again with the useful resource of within the route of the semester in comparison to the finals, so every mark you get proper here will lessen stress for the final crunch. As a result, it is critical to reach the ones to do well within the route. Fortunately, the techniques for every are very comparable, and with an try now not difficult to understand.

For those checks, it's far of utmost significance to apprehend the material properly. Often there are closing dates, so you need to be able to take into account factors short. Cramming clogs your brief-term reminiscence, so it's far masses better to start reviewing lots in advance than the night time time earlier than the assessment. As extended as you aren't falling in the lower back of with the path time desk, making equipped early need to not be hard. Furthermore, beginning early may also offer you with time to artwork on any idea which you are struggling with. Due to the numerous blessings of starting to test early, you may be an entire lot extra prepared for fulfillment in case you achieve this.

While expertise the content material cloth fabric is beneficial, being able to use it on shape a solution is critical. This is what makes practicing vital, in particular doing the paintings yourself. It is straightforward to experience that you recognize what is going on whilst studying an instance in the textbook, but that may match away you clueless at the same time as you are on your personal finally of an evaluation. Stay a long way from the answers supplied at the side of a "workout test" or similar cloth, till you have got have been given made a right attempt on the query. Another accurate idea is to art work on any "exercise check" or similar material underneath sports as near the real problem as viable. This is composed of getting a time restriction, no longer using any unauthorized material (textbook, notes, calculators), and strolling in a quiet area. Practice makes fine, and that applies to assessments, so with the try, you may get the marks you desire.

In addition, it's miles critical to stay calm at a few level inside the evaluation. Reassure your self which you are prepared, even in case you enjoy you are not. Panicking will now not make some component a whole lot less complex it'll make it even greater difficult to attention and make you greater at risk of mistakes. Taking a few deep breaths may even assist calm your nerves. Remember that you have installed numerous attempt, and not something can forestall you from acing the check.

Time can play a exquisite characteristic in checks. As a quit end result, staying nicely-paced is important. Consider wherein the marks are whilst allocating it sluggish, do not get slowed down in locations with restricted marks. Finishing with time left is generally on hand, as you want to test your paintings as heaps as possible. If you finish with at least one-region of the allocated time remaining, try to redo the take a look at on scrap paper without looking at your earlier solutions, as you are a protracted manner much more likely to trap a mistake this manner. You have to take advantage of the time allotted, and keep away from leaving early, as you'll now not get a few distinct hazard to earn marks that may be lost to errors.

Acing your midterms, quizzes or tests is capacity. All it calls for is an effort in getting to know and using the material, similarly to believing you may do it. As prolonged as you try your fantastic, you need to be able to be triumphant, and each mark earned in a few unspecified time inside the future of the semester is lots a lot much less wanted at the examination.

The Final Boss: Acing the Final

Exams can be the maximum critical challenge inside the path. The greater strain of its significance, at the side of the reality that it is more in-intensity, and likely extra difficult, can all take a toll on morale. However, much like exams, midterms, assignments and quizzes, succeeding on the examination are practicable, with some attempt.

The first step is to not relax too early. Any smash after weeks of schooling, labs, tutorials, homework and assignments may additionally moreover seem tempting to apply for rest. However, you truly ought to no longer permit the semester whole of hard art work visit waste via manner of beneath making geared up for the exam. Now isn't always the time to ease off the accelerator, as a substitute it's time to location the pedal to the metallic. Consider that your put up-exam break may be an lousy lot greater amusing in case you recognize you had been a achievement inside the assessments. As a stop end result, it's far vital to preserve the momentum going thru the exams, like how a runner does no longer sluggish down just in advance than the stop line.

Studying for exams is similar to reading for a midterm, however with extra content. This makes prioritizing a whole lot extra vital, as you can't spend time reviewing the whole thing at maximum depth. Focusing on your weaknesses is a extremely good approach, as a chain is best as robust as its weakest link. However, do no longer overestimate your strengths every, as you may get rusty on those through the years, which might also harm your common typical performance on the very last too. Also, maintain in mind how loads cloth is from every unit or problem be counted, as some additives may additionally additionally moreover have extra significance, and this is usually explicitly described by the teacher. The more content cloth manner that you can not cover the whole lot to its fullest, so that you need to pay interest on regions wherein it's far wanted most.

Exams can blend techniques that you did now not see ultimately of the path. This is why it's miles crucial to have the capacity to place the entirety you placed collectively. There may be just a few questions that don't cover single sections, or there may be many. In addition, there may be questions that incorporate extending your data. This makes it an wonderful idea to artwork with questions that encompass multiple property you learned. Such questions are likely to be on exercise assessments, but also can be placed in examination assessment additives of the textbook. Being organized to area topics together can help masses all through the exam.

The examination is the very last detail that can prevent you from getting the marks you need. Therefore, placing the try in will save you regret in a while, and you will be capable of have a nicely-earned harm afterwards.

Chapter 14: Choose Your Professors Wisely

Grade inflation, the phenomenon whereby teachers assign higher grades to students than they did inside the past, is nicely-documented inside the US and awesome countries round the arena. ACT, for instance, the non-earnings that administers standardized college readiness exams, decided that the common immoderate university GPA within the US extended from three.17 in 2010 to a few.36 in 2021.[1] In addition, the not unusual GPA at four-yr colleges and universities country wide accelerated from ~2.Eighty five in 1983, to ~three in 1998, to ~3.15 in 2013.[2]

Numerous factors may be in the back of a international upward thrust in grade inflation. On the macro, better grades represent better commencement prices, which is probably suitable for universities and might translate to higher university beauty charges for excessive college university students. On the micro, teachers who assign higher grades will be predisposed to get hold of higher pupil critiques. Similarly, departments with a reputation for grade inflation can entice better enrollment. This improvement bears many hallmarks of a classical "race to the lowest," in which stakeholders experience obligated to inflate their grades to stay competitive with their friends. On the opportunity hand, a few critics feature grade inflation to a broader societal fashion towards entitlement and anti-competitiveness (the "participation trophy era"). A sweeping claim like this is hard to evaluate, however I do agree with that teachers who grew up in an generation of grade inflation are more likely reachable out higher grades to their respective college college college students.

Grade inflation varies now not only among establishments, however among departments of the same establishments and among professors of the identical departments. Some departments oblige professors to grade on a bell curve in which a hard and speedy percentile of college students in every elegance get preserve of As, Bs, and Cs. Other departments are more open-ended, in which case grading is on the handiest discretion of the teacher. While excessive college college college college students are limited in phrases of what teachers they could take, most university packages feature a menu of options for primary and loose non-compulsory courses. It is frequently viable to avoid a particular professor you don't need to take a category with and make certain which you take a category taught by using manner of way of some other one with whom you do.

Several issues have advantage in a scholar's choice whether or not or not to join a class, together with essential necessities, direction contents, the professor's experience and coaching fashion, and scheduling consolation. However, in case your intention is to maximize your GPA, you may upload grading trouble to the pinnacle of the listing. Grading trouble isn't always to be burdened with the difficulty of the material itself. Just because of the truth a class is a breeze, that doesn't advise the instructor will assign many As. And virtually due to the fact a class is difficult, that doesn't recommend the instructor has a queue of university students organized to fail.

You can discover a professor's grading popularity through the usage of way of speaking to superb students. In addition, RateMyProfessors.Com, which helps

American, Canadian, and British establishments, stays the gold famous on questions of grading problem and easy professor satisfactory. Some professors outsource grading to Teaching Assistants (TAs), in which case grading for their courses can be unpredictable. However, TAs stay under the direction of professors, who reserve the proper to implement curves and regulate grades as preferred. While some professors wash their arms of grading selections, TA grading behavior often mirror a professor's possibilities in times in which departmental grading is discretionary.

In my six years of college, I took training with professors that graded on a strict bell curve; instructions wherein eighty%+ of college college students had been given an A; and training which embody 10-20 university college students in which only one pupil have been given an A. As a protracted manner as I may want to tell, grading averages had a good deal less to do with magnificence preferred overall performance and more to do with the habits of man or woman professors and departments.

When I become an undergraduate, Georgetown delivered a characteristic in which university college college students can get right of entry to the imply grades for their publications on the stop of every semester. This facts have emerge as enlightening, every in phrases of grade inflation and relative instructional prevalent overall performance. If your university discloses advocate grades, you could request this records from fellow classmates and element them into your choice whether to take a in addition beauty with a professor you had within the beyond.

Finally, a few professors and instructions are more dogmatic than others. If you're a staunch capitalist, suitable achievement getting an A in a class taught via a fanatical communist. Professors with sturdy non-public biases may additionally moreover moreover conflate struggle of phrases with misconception and/or terrible instructional typical performance. In my revel in, maximum teachers attempt to be objective, but I wouldn't take my opportunities in times in which they've got a reputation to the other.

In sum, most grade inflation starts offevolved by using taking commands taught through way of professors who are notorious for passing out As like candy. Your first undertaking as a four.0-aspiring scholar is to investigate your instructors earlier and construct your schedule as a end result.

Review the Syllabus

"The syllabus is the terms and conditions of a class that few university students have a look at however all are project to."

We live in a bureaucratic age in which severa administrative and authorities abilties entail meticulous documentation. Enter elegance syllabi. At remarkable, a syllabus is a constitution. At worst, it is a treasured guidepost and gameplan containing applicable records. The syllabus tells you methods an lousy lot distinct necessities will weigh inside the final grade equation.

Participation is probably well worth 30% of the very last grade for one elegance, while only 10% – or even plenty less – for some other. If you ever want to make a alternate-off in effort and time committed to a selected assignment, the syllabus have to inform that preference. For example, a research paper really worth 40% of the final grade clearly warrants greater training than a midterm well really worth excellent 15%. Keep in mind that syllabi are regulated with the useful resource of manner of departments and inform enrollment alternatives, and instructors usually adhere to them with a excessive degree of precision.

Syllabi regularly contain the grading rubric for essential assignments. A grading rubric for a paper assignment could likely encompass writing fashion, clarity of verbal exchange, proof of studies, cope with of counterarguments, citations, and creativity. Teachers and Teaching Assistants normally have many college students in addition to numerous research, administrative, and educational responsibilities. They also can spend ten minutes assigning a grade to a paper that took you ten hours to install writing, and the rubric tells you exactly what they may be going to be seeking out inside the direction of that span. While wondering outdoor the sphere is a terrific skills to have in life, disregarding the rubric is a surefire manner to get a lousy grade. An A-degree submission in line with one grading rubric might also additionally render a failing grade on any other.

Finally, past due outcomes are a notorious GPA killer. Amid instructional and life chaos, it's easy to lose music of very last dates for assignments, it's far why copying them down from the syllabus to a unique region is typically endorsed. Nothing brings a stellar A-submission right all of the way right down to a B or C quicker than a late penalty.

Tip #2 is proof that intelligence, and every so often even artwork ethic, are overestimated in terms of doing well in faculty. Having super organizational talents and following suggestions, which honestly all and sundry is capable of, can prevent unforced mistakes that degrade instructional overall performance.

Chapter 15: Attend Class Consistently

A prerequisite to success in any in any project is "showing up," and lessons are not any exception. (Mark Tomforde, PhD)[3]

During the educational 365 days, attending beauty is the unmarried biggest factor any student can do to get better grades. Students who do now not attend beauty regularly rarely ever get As, and college students who do get As aren't frequently ever absent. There are myriad reasons, tangible and in any other case, why that is the case.

First, a whole lot of instructors take attendance and take a look at participation. I've taken schooling wherein participation comprised five% of the final grade, and others wherein the decide changed into as immoderate as 30%. Participation is "low-placing fruit" for individuals who attend magnificence, even as not attending splendor is the very exquisite manner to shoot yourself in the foot. If you cast off not anything else from this Nerd's Guide, certainly visit beauty and desire for the splendid.

Second, inside the 50+ university instructions I've taken, tests nearly generally included material explicitly drawn from lectures. Indeed, lectures generally tend to are anticipating checks plenty better than readings, that may experience like a considerable sea to navigate. In addition, professors are recognised to move over material in lectures that isn't located within the readings, which university college students are at risk of be examined on. While you may get notes from a chum (See Tip #10), attending magnificence your self is the advanced-fireside manner to gather everything you want to understand. When we attend elegance, we additionally store time through manner of having our questions spoke back and receiving clues and steerage that would inform our education.

Third, and possibly most importantly, attendance is evidence of personal investment in a class. When a pupil suggests hobby in doing properly, a professor is much more likely to work with them to attain their intention. Attending class is likewise a sign of understand. It communicates that the pupil values what the professor has to say, whilst a loss of attendance can be visible as disrespectful. Most professors don't like giving out terrible grades. Bad grades discourage college college students, purpose horrible trainer evaluations, and create interpersonal tension. However, on the identical time as a scholar doesn't regularly attend class, relaxation assured they won't assume times.

Finally, a grade is a performance assessment for a selected beauty, not a median scenario depend. If you get an A+ in East Asian History, that does not suggest you're an expert in East Asian History. Nor does failing Statistics advocate you are incompetent at math. A magnificence, alternatively, is narrowly defined through way of a syllabus and includes a hard and rapid substantial sort of stay periods and unbiased assignments. In sum, getting appropriate grades is prepared immersing oneself in beauty data, it without a doubt is best feasible with regular attendance.

Sit inside the Front of the Classroom

"Students within the the the front of the magnificence are regularly greater in tune with the trainer, which interprets into taking extra notes, taking element extra in class discussions, and preserving higher take a look at behavior. All this typically translates right into a higher grade." (Robert Wallace)[4]

The interest of university college students in a lecture room is directed within the course of the teacher. And a instructor, like severa human beings, has the remarkable hobby of the folks that are closest to them. As a quit result, sitting toward the the the front will growth visibility and presence close to instructors and different university college students. This responsibility translates to a heightened hobby and elevates the stakes of having distracted. There is an expression, "Out of sight, out of mind." It is commonly actual that the similarly we're faraway from a person or some component, the lots much less of our interest it captures. Due to those social and physiological elements, college students who sit down down within the the the front of the elegance take in more records. Sitting inside the the front is also a social cue which you are keen to research, and teachers like to praise this form of scholar with an A.

The temptation to get distracted is double inside the computer age. If you've ever sat within the decrease returned of a big lecture hall, you understand exactly what I'm speaking approximately. I've visible people playing video games, surfing the net, looking sports sports highlights, working on photo layout obligations, and whispering to their pals. And I've been all the ones human beings at notable junctures. This shape of slacking off isn't in fact reserved to massive lecture halls. It additionally affects university college students in an lousy lot smaller school rooms with 20-50 college students. Unless the instructor has everyone sitting in a circle or roundtable, there can be a dating among in which a student chooses to take a seat and their diploma of interest. The quantity to that you are much more likely to get referred to as on for sitting near the the the front is the identical extent to which the instructor is noticing your funding within the elegance.

If your goal is to get the very quality possible grade, you've already received 1/2 of of the battle genuinely with the useful resource of the usage of displaying as a great deal as beauty. Sitting in the the the front, which doesn't require any unique intelligence or art work ethic, is the subsequent logical step to make the most out of it slow.

Chapter 16: Take Prolific Notes

There is a pronouncing, "Better is a quick pencil than an extended memory." The human reminiscence, for all its famed exploits, is concurrently fragile. On the opportunity hand, writing can seize facts exactly and because it must be. There's an expression in Arabic, "The donkey learns through repetition" (Al-takraar, bi3allim al Himaar). A lot of eloquence receives out of region in translation, however I anticipate there can be a parallel. Students who maintain the maximum records don't constantly have a photographic memory, however they do have a addiction of taking appropriate notes.

When I even have turn out to be an undergraduate, ~75% of students brough a laptop to schooling that have been statistics-rich and in the essential word-based totally (facts, philosophy, political technological information, and so forth.).

On the alternative hand, a conventional notebook can also but be most high quality for math, economics, and smaller language/communicate classes which is probably slight on notes and for which generation may be a distraction. Whenever it's far sensible to perform that, I appreciably suggest bringing a computer to class because of the reality a professional typist can churn out text as a minimum times as efficaciously as a hand-creator. Faster transcription portions to extra latest notes and plenty much less time and strength squandered on the logistics of moving text to the paper/show. (For more at the benefits of velocity typing, see Tip #15 entitled "Learn How To Type Faster").

Bottom line: Unless our teacher tells us, we do now not apprehend what statistics might be relevant for an examination, consequently the more prolific notes we take the higher organized we are to excel.

Participate in Classroom Discussion and Ask Questions

Teachers are experts in their respective fields. They are also experts approximately their expectations for assignments. When we take part in elegance and ask questions, we benefit insight into every. Active engagement allows focus. Some teachers call on college college students randomly to preserve them on their toes. On the other hand, by means of the usage of approach of selecting to take part, we prompt the equal effect in ourselves independent of our teachers' pedagogic style. While a few university college students sit up straight for an epiphany to elevate their hands, the bar for making a meaningful contribution to the elegance is quite low. If we are paying hobby all through lecture and appealing simply with the readings on our very personal time, then which include to speak calls for most effective a minimal quantity of intentionality and forethought. Active engagement is proof of intellectual hobby, it is the hallmark of an informed mind.

As I addressed in Tip #three on attending elegance, participation is a grading criterion of many publications, and that is composed of each attendance and active engagement in examine room speak. This concrete price, regardless of the truth that it most effective constitutes 5-10% of the final grade, isn't always negligible. On the opportunity hand, participation gives college college students the opportunity to reveal initiative. As a student for 20+ years from preschool thru graduate college, I positioned that instructors have a dependancy of profitable attempt and mindset, similarly to the standard gain-primarily based completely absolutely normal normal overall performance. In specific terms, whilst instructors see that a pupil is giving most strive, they'll be more likely to offer them an high-quality grade. Even half of a letter grade is a large payoff for doing simply one issue that can be compounded through enforcing a number of the alternative strategies mentioned in this book.

Not everybody is comfortable speaking in magnificence, and it could take a piece of courage to speak up. If, for anything cause, Tip #6 truly isn't your jam, you can constantly meet with a professor earlier than or after elegance. In addition, I'd advocate availing yourself of the following Tip #7.

Go To Office Hours

"Attending place of work hours, whether or not or no longer in character or online, can come up with treasured time to better recognize your elegance content material cloth and your professor's expectancies and might have a huge impact for your academic achievement." (The Learning Center, UNC Chapel Hill)[5]

Office hours are at the same time as instructors make themselves to be had to fulfill with college college students outside of sophistication to speak about direction fabric, assignments, grades, and actually a few other trouble depend number associated with academia and "the actual global." Even if we assume we're doing well in a category, meeting with instructors is a sensible technique. Educators have spent years analyzing and education their scenario and understand the syllabus/applicable readings indoors-out. Direct remarks from the author of an assignment can be useful at some point of its execution. Conferring with our teachers maintains us from erring and lets in us to accurate our errors earlier than it's miles too late. In times wherein we are on the right music, to be advised "preserve doing what you're doing" can provide us the information to stay the direction with a selected concept, strategy, or argument. Every time I met with teachers in high college or college to speak approximately an drawing near undertaking, I got here away higher located to ace it. All college students stand to benefit some thing with the beneficial resource of going to place of work hours. Full save you.

www.ingramcontent.com/pod-product-compliance
Lightning Source LLC
Chambersburg PA
CBHW071440080526
44587CB00014B/1929